Local History
and
Genealogy Abstracts
from

# *Fairmount News*

Fairmount, Indiana

1888–1900

*Ralph D. Kirkpatrick*

HERITAGE BOOKS
2011

# HERITAGE BOOKS
*AN IMPRINT OF HERITAGE BOOKS, INC.*

**Books, CDs, and more—Worldwide**

For our listing of thousands of titles see our website
at
www.HeritageBooks.com

Published 2011 by
HERITAGE BOOKS, INC.
Publishing Division
100 Railroad Ave. #104
Westminster, Maryland 21157

Copyright © 1997 Ralph D. Kirkpatrick

All rights reserved. No part of this book may be reproduced or transmitted in any form or by any means, electronic or mechanical, including photocopying, recording or by any information storage and retrieval system without written permission from the author, except for the inclusion of brief quotations in a review.

International Standard Book Numbers
Paperbound: 978-0-7884-0653-9
Clothbound: 978-0-7884-8626-5

# FOREWORD

North Carolina Quakers, escaping the moral blight of a southern society based on human slavery, settled the area near the site of Fairmount along Back Creek in the late-1820's and early 1830's. Families named Winslow, Hill, Newby, Baldwin, Rush, Benbow, Morris, and Harvey were prominant among the early settlers. Other settlers followed and the dense forests and wet prairies were gradually converted to agricultural production. Schools and churches were established and developed. The town of Fairmount located on Back Creek in Fairmount Township, Grant County, Indiana was established and named by Quakers in the mid-nineteenth century. The town was named for the beautiful 'Fairmount Park' in the Quaker City of Philadelphia, Pennsylvania. The Civil War claimed the attention of the community and also claimed the lives of several who died in the northern army. Growth of the town and its population following the war was slow but quickened with the coming of the railroads. Natural gas discoveries and gas exploitation dominated the 1890's. Factorys, particularly glass factorys, were built to utilize the gas.

Newspapers chronicled the births, marriages and deaths in the community. The movements of persons to the West or to other places were also noted. All existing Fairmount newspapers published through 1900 were gleaned for the following abstracts.

## Abbreviations and conventions used:
anniv - anniversary
att - attends or attended
b - born in or date of birth
BC - Back Creek
bldg. - building
bur - buried at
ca - circa; about
Cem - Cemetery
Ch. - Church
Coll - College
Co. - County (county name not followed by a state name is an Indiana county)
CW - Civil War
d - died on
dec - deceased
dt - daughter of
f - former or formerly

FFA - Fairmount Friends Academy
Fmt. - Fairmount
GAR - Grand Army of the Republic, Civil War veterans organization
grad - graduate or graduate of
HS - High School
m - married
mbr - member of
M.E. - Methodist Episcopal Church
mgr. - manager
MH - Meetinghouse; building used for religious services
mi. - mile or miles
M/M - Mr. and Mrs.
M.P. - Methodist Protestant Church
(Name) - maiden name of married woman or widow
'Name' - nickname
Name - name this person was known by or 'went by'
[Name or other data] - explanatory data not from Fairmount News
prob - probably
prop. - proprietor
RR - railroad
s - son of
Sch - School
serv - served in
SS - Sunday School
tchr - teacher
Twp. - Township
U.B. - United Brethren Church
vet - veteran or veteran of
WCTU - Women's Christian Temperance Union
wk - week
W.M. - Wesleyan Methodist Church
yr - year or years

Ralph D. Kirkpatrick, Ph.D.<br>
Osage Farm

LOCAL HISTORY AND GENEALOGY ABSTRACTS FROM "FAIRMOUNT NEWS", FAIRMOUNT, INDIANA, 1888-1900

ACHOR, Daniel - of near Roseburg; age 70; d 3 Aug 1900 (8/9/00)

ADAMS, Iz - of Jonesboro, 21 Jun 1899 was killed in a hunting accident (6/22/99)

ADAMS, Mrs. Tamer - see Mahlon BREWER

ADDISON, Silas E. - of 4 mi. W of Fmt.; b Rush Co. ca Dec 1858; s Linden H. and Eliza Ann; came to Grant Co. 1879; m Josephine Hockett 20 Jul 1884; d 15 Jun 1900, bur Park Cem (6/28/00)

ALBERT, B.F. - and George Collins contract to build White Egg Friends MH (3/12/91)

ALBERT, Frank - Liberty Twp. Trustee (3/24/92)

ALBERT, Zadie - age ca 22; dt Frank Albert of Hackleman; d 11 Jan 1900, bur Park Cem (1/11/00)

ALBRIGHT, Rev. __ - pastor of Salem Ch. (9/10/91)

ALEXANDER, Elijah H. - lives in Fmt.; serv Co. I, 130th Regmt. Ind. Vol. Inf. during CW (9/15/92); att CW vet Reunion in Elwood (8/7/96)

ALEXANDER, Harry - age 2 yr; s M/M A.C. Alexander; d 2 Jan 1891 (1/8/91)

ALLEN, infant - child of M/M Newt Allen; d 22 Aug 1900 (8/23/00)

ALLEN, infant - b recently; s M/M Eli Allen of N of Fmt. (10/11/00)

ALLEN, Newt - buys out his Palace Meat Market partner, Elwood Haisley (10/13/92); sold his Fmt. meat market to H.W. Dickinson (4/19/00)

ALLEN, Saphrona - a Summitville pioneer; wife of Reuben Allen; d 30 Nov 1889 (12/5/89)

ALLRED, Clarence Raymond - b 23 Jun 1900; s Oscar and Bell; d 3 Aug 1900 (8/16/00)

ALLRED, David E. - and wife have dt, b 4 Apr 1889 (4/11/89); is painting contractor (4/25/89); 1871, came to Fmt. area; owns grocery store; operates a delivery wagon in Fmt. (4/14/92); is painting and wallpapering Dr. J.W. Patterson's new residence (4/22/98)

ALLRED, Elizabeth J. - b Randolph Co., NC 2 Apr 1820; m Moses Allred 16 Nov 1843; mbr W.M. Ch.; d Fmt. 10 Feb 1892 (2/11/92; 2/18/92)

ALLRED, George N. - lives at Rigdon (9/15/92); Fmt. area CW vet of Co. K, 130th Ind. Vol. Inf. att his Unit Reunion in Elwood (8/7/96)

ALLRED, Lawana Ruth - b 30 Aug 1896; dt Oscar and Bell Allred; d 6 Aug 1897, funeral in BC Friends MH, bur Park Cem (8/20/97)

ALLRED, Moses - CW vet bur BC Friends Cem (5/23/89; 6/5/96); d ca 1872 (2/18/92)

ALLRED, Oscar - s Charles Allred; m Bell (8/20/97)

AMMERMAN, Dora Cecil - b 4 Jun 1891; s Lagrand and Mary; d 9 Oct 1897, bur BC Friends Cem (10/15/97)

ANDREWS, Georgia May - b 7 Aug 1887; dt Laban and Josie Andrews; mbr Bethel M.P. Ch.; d 18 Feb 1899 (3/2/99)

ANDREWS, Josie - see Josie DeLONG

ANDREWS, Laban - m Josie; d ca 1888 (3/2/99)

ANDRICK, Frank - Asst. Supt., Bell Window Glass Factory (11/29/00)

ARMSTRONG, P.C. - mbr, Fmt. Gun Club (9/21/99)

ARMSTRONG, Roscoe - 1896 grad, Green Twp. Schs (6/5/96)

ARNETT, Annis - see Annis SCOTT

ARNETT, Lin - landowner near Fmt. advertising that he permits no hunting on his property (11/12/97)

ARNETT, Mahala C. (Humbard) - d Fmt. 26 Jul 1892 (7/28/92); b 14 Feb 1836; dt __ Humbard; m 1st in Jun 1850 William Elliott (dec Nov 1862); m 2nd 23 Aug 1863 Elwood Arnett (dec); mbr W.M. Ch. (8/4/92)

ARNOLD, Malissa J. - see Joseph Mansfield Bradford

ASKINS, George - age 11 months; s M/M Monroe Askins; d 30 Jul 1900 (8/1/00)

ASPY, Rev. Lotus - Fmt. Baptist Ch. pastor (3/27/96; 2/5/97); recently ordained as a Baptist Minister (5/22/96)

ASPY, Rev. T.A. - of Greensburg; brother of Rev. L. Aspy (4/17/96)

ATKINSON, Cora E. - see William THOMAS

ATKINSON, Ellsworth - att DePauw Univ (3/11/98)

AUSTIN, C.E. - left this wk for KS to help thresh wheat (6/28/00)

BACK CREEK - John Kelsay, Fmt. Twp. Trustee, says ditch assessments for this creek are now due (10/6/92); creek is to be widened to 26 feet and made 30 inches deep (11/3/92); creek is to be cleaned out again (8/23/00)

BACK CREEK FRIENDS CEMETERY - 2 bodies were recently taken from here and re-buried in Park Cem (6/13/89); Improvement Committee mbrs are: James Nixon, Eli Thomas, Daniel Whybrew, J.K. Pemberton, R.S. Wilson, Q. Baldwin, Jesse Jay, and E. Newby (9/1/92); is free cem in that anyone can use it for burial without plot charge (1/24/96); Union veterans of CW burials include: Jacob M. Martin, A.G. Little, Thomas Cox, Harry Dean, Thomas Wilson, William Jay, Jonathan Smithson, Charles Carey, Jacob McCoy, J.D.

Lewis, John Gibson, Alfred Waldron, Alex Pickard, John Buller, Joseph Rush, Moses Allred and Gilmore Hollingsworth (6/5/96)

BAILEY, Benjamin S. - Fmt. carpenter (4/14/92); contractor for 8 or 9 yr; skipped town 28 Jun 1900 leaving his 8 motherless children and numerous debts (7/5/00); is in St. Paul, Minne. (8/23/00)

BAILEY, Mrs. Benjamin S. - age 48; m; d 6 Apr 1900 (4/12/00)

BAILEY, Captolea J. - see Captolea Jennie MIDDLETON

BAILEY, Susan - 3 Aug 1897 d at Hackleman (8/6/97)

BAKER, Anna - see Oliver SCOTT

BAKER, Carl - s John Baker (7/2/97)

BAKER, John S. - Fmt. builder & contractor (5/16/89); is in business with J.B. Smithson (4/14/92)

BAKER, Maggie - 1899-1900 Fmt. HS tchr (8/24/99)

BAKER, Mary E. - age 38y, 7m; dt S.A. Baker; d 24 Oct 1892, bur Park Cem (10/27/92)

BAKER, S.A. - Fmt. CW vet; Beeson Post, GAR, Adjutant (4/18/89)

BALDWIN, __ - see Mrs. A.E. STANLEY

BALDWIN, __ - b 31 Jan 1896; s M/M Daniel Baldwin (2/7/96)

BALDWIN, A.M. - plans to make a summer resort at Lake Galatia with rowboats, a steam launch, and a small hotel (6/25/97)

BALDWIN, Anna - see Anna FELLOW

BALDWIN, Asa T. - taught sch in fall, 1867 (10/17/89); of Marion; s Thomas and Lydia (5/25/99)

BALDWIN, Charles - prominent early settler in Fmt. Twp. (1/7/92)

BALDWIN, Daniel - prominent early settler in Fmt. Twp. (1/7/92)

BALDWIN, David - b Wayne Co. 6 Nov 1819; s Daniel and Christina; came to Fmt. Twp. 1833; m Elizabeth Coleman 29 Jan 1846; had no children; mbr M.E. Ch.; d 3 Feb 1898, bur Park Cem (2/4/98; 2/11/98)

BALDWIN, Edgar M. - employed by U.S. Printing Office, Washington, D.C.; writes a Washington column for Fmt. News (10/22/91); Pvt., 160th Ind. Regmt. (11/3/98); is in camp at Columbus, GA (1/12/99)

BALDWIN, Elizabeth 'Libbie' (Coleman) - widow of David Baldwin (2/4/98; 2/11/98); lives with her nephew Dr. J.W. Patterson and his family on E. Washington St. (6/3/98)

BALDWIN, Emaline (Tuttle) - sister of James Tuttle of Fmt.; d at her home near Marion 30 May 1896 (6/5/96)

BALDWIN, Hannah - widow of Elias Baldwin; d 18 May 1896 in her Fmt. home, bur Park Cem (5/22/96)

BALDWIN, Joseph - age 73; gave Fmt. its name; lives on Main Street (1/7/92)

BALDWIN, L.D. - Marion attorney; applies for divorce from his wife, Margaret (1/26/99)

BALDWIN, Landy - Fmt. soldier serving in Philippines, is returning home with 20th Kansas Regmt. (9/21/99)

BALDWIN, Lydia - of Marion; b Wayne Co. 25 Dec 1814; m Thomas Baldwin, Sep 1833; moved to site of Fmt., 1834; mbr Friends; d 21 May 1899, has double funeral with dec husband, bur Marion IOOF Cem (5/25/99)

BALDWIN, Lydia Jane (Stanfield) - b Green Co., TN 12 Nov 1823; dt David and Elizabeth Stanfield; 16 Apr 1850 m Joseph W. Baldwin; mbr Friends; d 7 Oct 1892, bur Marion IOOF Cem (10/13/92)

BALDWIN, Mary - see Charles Verling MOORE

BALDWIN, Micah - and Seth Cox have a Fmt. Shoe Shop (10/15/91); came to Fmt. area ca 1833; repairs boots and shoes in his shop (4/14/92)

BALDWIN, Minnie - see Minnie DELEAMP

BALDWIN, Orlando F. - Pvt., 20th Kansas Regmt.; is fighting 23 mi. from Manila, Philippines (6/1/99)

BALDWIN, Quincy - mbr BC Friends Cem Improvement Committee (9/1/92)

BALDWIN, S.G. - of Marion; s Thomas and Lydia (5/25/99)

BALDWIN, Sarah - mbr Fmt. Friends Women's Foreign Missionary Society (11/26/91)

BALDWIN, Terah - of Marion; s Thomas and Lydia (5/25/99)

BALDWIN, Thomas - of Marion; b Wayne Co. 26 Apr 1813; m Lydia in Sep 1833; moved to site of Fmt., 1834; mbr Friends; d 25 May 1899, has double funeral with dec wife, bur Marion IOOF Cem (5/25/99)

BALLENGER, Edna - grad FFA 1899; att Univ of Wisconsin (1/25/00)

BALLINGER, Ed - of Upland d 10 Sep 1892 (9/15/92)

BANNISTER, Amos - 25 Dec 1898 m Flora Wells; both of Liberty Twp. (12/29/98)

BARGER, Edward B. - age 44; m; d 21 Apr 1900, bur Waynesville, OH (4/26/00; 5/3/00); widow Eva will stay in Fmt. (5/24/00)

BARR, Daisy - wife of Thomas Barr; Friends Minister; is holding revival at Linwood Friends MH (3/19/97)

BARR, T.D. - tchr, Monroe Twp. Sch No. 10 (11/14/89)

BARREN CREEK - oak timber extended along this Fmt. Twp. creek in 1829 when first settlers came (1/7/92); Barren Creek gas well sent out fire and roared last Sat. night (8/4/92); it is proposed to ditch Lake Galatia into Barren Creek (11/17/92)

BARRETT, Mrs. Levi - lived in Fmt. near FFA; d 14 Feb 1900, bur Windfall cem (2/15/00)

BASSETT, Lillian P. - 1899-1900 Fmt. HS tchr (8/24/99)

BATES, Os - Fmt. soldier serving in Philippines (9/21/99)

BEALS, Emma - mbr Fmt. W.M. SS (9/26/89)

BEALS, Enoch - May 1862 enlisted in Co. K, 1st Ind. Cav. (9/26/89; 1/28/92); officer in Beeson Post, GAR (12/10/91); b Greene Co., TN 14 Oct 1841; m; d 22 Jan 1892 (1/28/92); bur in Park Cem (6/5/96)

BEALS, Jacob - owns the Eagle Shoe Store in Fmt. (5/16/89); b TN, came to Fmt. in 1873 (4/14/92); moved his shoe shop to bldg. across the street N from Flanagan's Store (3/4/98)

BEALS, Mollie - mbr Fmt. Women's Relief Corps (11/14/89)

BEALS, Newt - given party 24 Feb 1889 for his 45th birthday (2/28/89)

BEALS, Robert J. - s Enoch Beals (1/28/92)

BEALS, Sarah - see Reuel JulianGAUNTT

BEASLEY, W.A. - mbr, Fmt. Gun Club (9/21/99); sells 'Banner Salve' (5/3/00)

BEASLEY, Will - owns/operates Beasley Drug Store (7/25/89), sells drugs, books, stationary, wallpaper, and paint (7/2/91)

BECKS, Silas L. - colored; a widower; Liberty Twp Dist. # 3 Sch tchr; d 11 Jan 1889 (1/17/89; 2/21/89)

BEESON, A. - owns Beeson Grocery Store (3/27/96)

BEIDLER, __ - child of William Beidler d 11 July 1889 (7/11/89)

BEIDLER, June A. - b 3 Jun 1886; dt J. William and Prudence Beidler; d 21 Nov 1897, bur Park Cem (11/26/97)

BEIDLER, Mabel - is att Oberlin Coll (10/4/00)

BEIDLER, Mary Hazel - age 3 yr; dt J. William and Prudence C. Beidler; d 24 Nov 1892 (11/24/92; 12/1/92)

BELL, James M. - Fmt. Friends bldg. committee mbr (2/11/92)

BERRY, Col. J.I. - can be hired to trim fruit trees, shade trees and vines (3/4/98)

BIDDLECUM, Homer - att North Grove Sch (2/26/97)

BIDDLECOME, Jason - is Postmaster at new Pansy post office (7/14/92); also has a blacksmith shop in Pansy (8/25/92)

BINFORD, Vashti - dt M/M B.H. Binford of Carthage; FFA tchr (4/9/97); is going to Paris Exposition (6/14/00)

BISHOP, Will - is in 160th Ind. Regmt. in a camp at Columbus, GA (1/12/99)

BIXBEY, Hattie - see Hattie WILSON

BLOOMER, J.M. - and A.W. Shuey own/operate a restaurant/boarding house in Fmt.; they purchased the restaurant from __ Galloway (4/14/92)

BOGUE, __ - age 2y, 7m; s Robert Bogue; burned to death last Saturday (1/4/00)

BOGUE, Amos H. - b Preble Co., OH 13 Apr 1833; s Charles and Sarah; m 1st __; m 2nd Elmina Scott 20 Mar 1883; came to Grant Co. ca 1872; mbr Friends; d 29 Jan 1900, bur Park Cem (2/1/00; 2/15/00)

BOGUE, Anne - age 20; dt M/M Thomas Bogue; grad-Marion HS 1886; d near Fmt. 2 Aug 1891 (8/6/91)

BOGUE, Burl - mbr Fmt. Friends boy's SS class (1/11/00)

BOGUE, Dora - dt Amos H. and Elmina (Scott) Bogue; FFA student (2/1/00; 2/15/00)

BOGUE, Elmina (Scott) - dt James Scott of Fmt. (1/18/00); m Amos H. Bogue 20 Mar 1883 (2/15/00)

BOGUE, Flora - see Frank MASON

BOGUE, Florence - see Florence MASON

BOGUE, Hazel - age 2y, 2m, 27da; dt Callie Bogue; d 5 Sept 1889 (9/12/89)

BOGUE, Helen - see Helen McWHARTER

BOGUE, Mrs. Jesse - of Archer, FL; dt Jonathan P. and Jane (Henley) Winslow (8/17/99; 8/24/99)

BOGUE, John - CW vet bur BC Friends Cem (5/23/89)

BOGUE, John - Charter Mbr, Fmt. Gun Club (6/26/96); brother of Exum Bogue of Fmt. and of Callie Bogue of Providence, IA (2/26/97)

BOGUE, Mary - see Phineus HENLEY

BOGUE, Mary Lavina - see Mary Lavina CAREY

BOGUE, Miss Nina - sister of W.D. Bogue (6/3/98)

BOGUE, Pearl - s Mrs. Robert Bogue (5/16/89); f mbr 4th Regmt. State Militia which merged into 160th Ind. Inf., was mustered out after fighting stopped in Cuba; is running for Grant Co. Recorder as a Republican (1/18/00)

BOGUE, Robert - of Fmt.; brother of Pearl Bogue and of Mrs. Millie Willey, both of Marion (10/29/91); d 27 Jun 1900 (6/28/00)

BOGUE, Thomas - paid $100.00 for a Shropshire sheep imported from England (11/12/91)

BOGUE, W.D. - Charter Mbr, Fmt. Gun Club (6/26/96); of Rising Sun, IN (6/3/98)

BOGUE, Mrs. Wilson - sister of Miss Leona Fink (1/18/00)

BOND, Mrs. Alva - d 21 Mar 1898 (4/1/98)

BOND, Amos - early Mill Twp. settler; d 28 Feb 1896 (3/6/96)

BOND, Mary - mbr Oak Ridge WCTU (6/3/98)

BORREY, John - and his 2 partners are starting the new Borrey Window Glass Factory (4/29/98); mgr. of Bell Window Glass Factory (12/1/98), and now resigns as mgr. (11/15/00)

BOWERS, Jake - glassblower for Dillon Glass Works (4/23/91)

BOWERS, Mrs. Martha - mbr Fmt. Rebecca Lodge 305 (1/11/00)

BOWERS, Samuel - of Cadiz, Henry Co; CW vet; visits J.B. Smithson, his old CW bunkmate (1/31/89; 12/31/91); serv Co. B, 130th Regmt. Ind. Vol. Inf. during CW (9/15/92)

BOWERS, William - electrician for LaRue electric plant; installed electric light plant at Zinc Smelting Works (4/20/99); Town of Fmt. hires him as electrician at $45 per month (6/22/99); is wiring new Borrey Blk. (9/20/00)

BOWMAN, Daniel W. - lived in Liberty Twp. for almost 50 yr; d 9 Nov 1897, funeral in Linwood Friends MH, bur Park Cem (11/12/97)

BOYD, Belle - famous Confederate spy, lectured in Fmt. Congregational Ch. 15 Mar 1899 (3/23/99)

BOYLAND, C.M. - a baker; is now a partner with McCandliss in Fmt. Restaurant & Bakery (8/11/92)

BRADFORD, Gertie A. - age 14; dt J. Mansfield and Malissa J. (Arnold) Bradford; att Little Ridge Sch (11/16/99)

BRADFORD, Joseph <u>Mansfield</u> - farmer; lived 2 mi. W of Fmt.; b 12 May 1863; s Otho and Sarah Bradford; 29 Dec 1883 m Malissa J. Arnold; mbr Friends; d 8 Nov 1899 (11/9/99; 11/16/99)

BRADFORD, Orpha E. - age 12; dt J. Mansfield and Malissa J. (Arnold) Bradford; att Little Ridge Sch (11/16/99)

BRANCH, Frank Graham - b 2 Oct 1846 New York, NY; s Henry E. and Emeline (Wilson); m; Supt., Indiana Natural Gas & Oil Co.; d 4 Mar 1900 in Columbia Hotel, bur Park Cem (3/8/00)

BRANCH, Rene O. - s Frank G. Branch; FFA student (3/8/00); mbr Fmt. Friends boy's SS class (1/11/00)

BRAND, Hattie - 1896 grad, Green Twp. sch (6/5/96)

BRATTAIN, C.D. - s Mrs. Anna Brattain (1/12/99)

BRECKENRIDGE, Margaret - see Margaret DAVIS

BRECKENRIDGE, Robert - of Knightstown; brother of Margaret (Breckenridge) Davis (dec) (11/16/99)

BREWER, Benjamin - CW vet bur in Park Cem (6/5/96)

BREWER, Lewis - leaves for KS to help thresh wheat (6/28/00)

BREWER, Mahlon - 11 Jul 1897 m Mrs. Tamer Adams (7/16/97)

BRIGGS, Rev. __ - leaves Center Christian Ch. pastorate (1/4/00)

BRILES, Charles S. - 1891-92 Oak Ridge Sch tchr (3/24/92); tchr, Pansy Sch 1892-93 (8/25/92); resigns as Pansy Sch tchr to be a clerk in the Jason Wilson Bank, Marion (10/13/92); b Fmt. Twp. Jul 1870; m 25 Mar 1896 Orpha LaPorte of Marion; d 3 Jul 1897 (7/9/97)

BRILES, E.E. - purchased the Fmt. Bowling Alley from W.W. Paddock (12/21/99)

BRILES, Jacob - s Lizzie Briles (12/27/88); b Randolph Co., NC 26 Oct 1844; has sawmill located 3.5 mi. SW of Fmt., employs 6 to 20 men (4/14/92)

BRILES, Jacob - lives in Yost, KY (11/5/97)

BRILES, Mrs. Jacob - and her sister, India Lawrence, are dressmakers on Penn St. (8/24/99)

BRILES, Nettie (McMaster) - of Swayzee; dt J.C. McMaster of Little Ridge area (2/14/96; 2/28/96); b near Fmt. 4 Aug 1872; dt J.C. and Nancy (dec 1891) McMaster; m Robert W. Briles 28 Apr 1894; mbr Christian Ch.; d 8/9 Mar 1896, bur BC Friends Cem (3/13/96)

BRILES, Robert W. - age ca 26; s M/M Jacob Briles; wife is dec; d 26 Oct 1897, funeral in BC Friends MH (11/5/97)

BROILES, Nelson - m; age 46; d 17 Dec 1898 after injury in a gas explosion on his farm SE of Fmt. (12/22/98)

BROOKS, Anna - see Anna HOLLINGSWORTH

BROOKS, Hannah J. - b 26 May 1876; dt John and Rebecca Brooks; d 19 Mar 1897, funeral in BC Friends MH, bur BC Friends Cem (3/26/97)

BROOKS, Lena - b 25 Apr 1896; dt John and Rebecca Brooks; d 27 Apr 1897 (4/30/97)

BROOKSHIRE, [Abigail] - see [Abigail] DeSELMS

BROOKSHIRE, Lizzie - dt Esquire Luther Brookshire (2/7/89); - see John T. McCOMBS

BROOKSHIRE, Morris - s Luther Brookshire; returned home after living in Arkansas for a time (4/10/96)

BROOKSHIRE, Thomas J. - serv 9th Ind. Cav. during CW (10/8/91)

BROWN, __ - see Mrs. David O. ICE

BROWN, infant - age 8 mon.; child of Dr./M C.N. Brown; d 18 Sep 1900 (9/20/00)

BROWN, Anna - Clark WILCUTS

BROWN, Annie Frances - see Annie Frances PILKENTON

BROWN, Bessie Beatrice - dt Robert Ray and Mary (Trueblood) Brown (4/27/99; 5/4/99); - see Bessie Beatrice HACKETT

BROWN, Dr. Charles N. - of Chicago; 1897 grad-Bennett Medical Coll, Chicago; was on House Staff of Cook Co. Hospital; purchases property on S. Main St.; to set up practice here (4/20/99); moves to Fmt. (5/11/99)

BROWN, James J. - employed by Norton's Store (7/25/89); now has a blacksmith shop (9/12/89; 4/14/92); head clerk in Frank Norton's new store in Fowlerton (7/31/96)

BROWN, Mrs. James - sister of William A. St. John (dec recently at Carmel, IL) (9/12/89)

BROWN, Dr. Karl Trueblood - 12 Apr 1899 grad Barnes' Medical Coll, St. Louis (4/13/99); s Robert Ray and Mary (Trueblood) Brown (4/27/99;5/4/99); now of Colborn, Tippecanoe Co. (11/16/99)

BROWN, Margaret Ann (Keith) - b Lincoln Co., TN 27 Mar 1837; m 23 May 1850 William A. Brown (dec 9 May 1894); came to Grant Co. in 1865; mbr Fmt. WCTU; d 5 Jun 1899 (6/8/99)

BROWN, Paul Deloss - s Robert Ray and Mary (Trueblood) Brown (4/27/99; 5/4/99)

BROWN, Robert Ray - b Salem 23 Mar 1834; s Samuel L. And Joanna Brown; 1 Jan 1857 m Mary Trueblood, dt Dr. Joshua Trueblood of Salem; lived in Westfield until 1891; during CW serv Co. E, 5th Cav., 90th Regmt.; mbr GAR; mbr Methodists; d Fmt. 26 Apr 1899 (4/27/99; 5/4/99)

BROWN, Ward Arnold - age 7y, 11m, 9da; s M/M William Brown; d 21 Dec 1897, bur Park Cem (12/24/97)

BROWN, William Arthur - of Marion; s Robert Ray and Mary (Trueblood) Brown (4/27/99; 5/4/99)

BROWN, William F. - Trustee, Fmt. Congregational Ch. (2/10/89); Cashier, Citizen's Exchange Bank (3/20/96)

BROWNING, Mary E. - see James SCOTT

BROYLES, Elizabeth - b KY 4 Jun 1812; Rush Co. 1834 m Thomas Gardner (dec 1850); m 2nd 1879 Handley Broyles (dec); mbr BC W.M. Ch.; lived 3 mi. SE of Fmt.; d 23 Jan 1897 (1/29/97)

BROYLES, Handley - b NC 20 Sep 1817; m Mrs. Elizabeth Gardner 10 Mar 1879; mbr BC W.M. Ch.; d 4 Mar 1896 (3/13/96)

BRUSH, G.A. - and W.M. Pogue own an electrical supply house (4/14/92)

BRYAN, Alvin D. - owner of hardware store (4/14/92); works as a tinner for J.W. Dale Hardware (3/11/98)

BRYAN, Earl - Charter Mbr, Fmt. Gun Club (6/26/96)

BRYAN, T.W. - works with brother, A.W. in hardware store (4/14/92)

BUCK, C.H. - of Fmt.; CW vet (3/28/89)

BULLER, B.F. - s Lindsey Buller; lives 2 mi. W of Fmt. (3/26/97)

BULLER, Charles - mbr Fmt. Friends boys' SS class (1/11/00)

BULLER, Chester Clarence - b 15 Apr 1892; s Oliver and Marta Buller; d 15 Feb 1898 (2/25/98)

BULLER, Clarence - grad FFA 1898 (1/11/00)

BULLER, Elizabeth - b Randolph Co., NC 7 Dec 1819; m Lindsey Buller; d at their home 1 mi. W of Fmt. 7 Sept 1891 (9/10/91)

BULLER, John - CW vet bur BC Friends Cem (5/23/89; 6/5/96)

BULLER, Lindsey - b Guilford Co., NC 29 Apr 1814; settled just E of site of Fmt. ca 1834, then entered government land 1.5 mi. W of Fmt.; m 1st Mary Lytle in 1835; m 2nd 25 Mar 1864 Elizabeth Freeman (dec 1891); joined BC W.M. Ch. ca 1858; d 21 Mar 1897, bur BC Friends Cem (3/26/97)

BULLER, Lydia A.C. [(Scott)]- of Liberty Twp. sues husband, John for divorce (12/21/99); asks court for living allowance (1/4/00)

BULLER, Mary - see George CARTER

BULLER, Minerva - widow of Clark Buller; d 27 Jul 1891, bur BC Friends Cem (7/30/91)

BULLER, Morton - is sued by Goldie Lewis for rape and for fathering her child, b 3 Jul 1900 (10/11/00)

BULLER, Oliver - leaves for KS to help thresh wheat (6/28/00)

BULLER, Sarah Ann (Wright) - dt Jacob Reese Wright; m B.F. Buller (2/19/97)

BULLER, Mrs. Thomas - dt Peter Thomas (6/21/00)

BULLINGER, F.A. - prop., Bakery & Restaurant (7/23/91; 4/14/92)

BULLINGER, Mrs. Flora A. - dt of Mrs. Sarah Pierce (1/7/92)

BUMPAS, Mrs. John H. - of Liberty Twp.; dt George J. And Sarah E. (Oldacre) Henshaw (1/5/99)

BURDEN, Mary - see William A. FRAZIER

BURNES, Demaris - see Nixon RUSH, Sr.

BURNS, John - CW vet living in New Cumberland; d 13 Aug 1892 (8/18/92)

BURWICK, J. - is mbr of a Fowlerton church (4/16/97)

BUSING, Mrs. Abbie - d 4 Nov 1891, bur Park Cem (11/5/91)

BUSING, Bessie - dt John and Abigail Busing (both dec); Joseph Pool is her guardian (4/17/96); - see Roll COOPER

BUSING, John - CW vet bur BC Friends Cem (5/23/89); his 'partially petrified' body was recently removed from BC Friends Cem for re-burial in Park Cem (12/24/91); CW vet now bur in Park Cem (6/5/96)

BUSING, John Rinehardt - s John and Abigail Busing (both dec); Joseph Pool is his guardian (4/17/96); 6 Dec 1899 is given party for his 27th birthday (12/7/99)

BUTLER, John W. - b Hancock Co. 25 May 1843; s George and Martha Butler of Fmt.; widower; of Marion; mbr Friends; d d 26 May 1889, bur BC Friends Cem (5/23/89; 5/30/89)

BUTLER, Mary J. - see Jasper N. WHEELER

BUTLER, Micajah - s George Butler of Fmt.; in past, taught in a Henry Co. Sch (11/21/89)

CALHOUN, Mrs. Laura E. - recently moved to Fmt. from Arkansas (12/19/89)

CALHOUN, William - now in Arkansas for his health; to teach in BC Sch this fall (4/18/89; 9/12/89); has large number of students in BC Sch (11/7/89); b Dayton, OH 24 yr ago; grad, BC Sch; att Marion Normal in spring 1883 (12/12/89); s Mrs. Laura E. Calhoun (12/19/89); resigns as FFA tchr to become a Sch Principal in Illinois (3/31/92)

CAIN, Frank - b Delaware Co. 16 Oct 1876; s Sarah Carpenter; step-s Henry Carpenter; d 25 Mar 1897 (4/2/97)

CALDWELL, Mrs. Eliza - of SW of Fmt.; d 15 Apr 1897, to be bur Park Cem (4/16/97)

CAMMACK, Bayard F. - d in his Marion home 30 Aug 1892 (9/1/92)

CAMMACK, Hazel - age 7; dt William T. and 'Emma' (Cox) Cammack (6/28/00; 7/12/00)

CAMMACK, Margaret Emler 'Emma' (Cox) - b 3 mi. SW of Fmt. 17 Jun 1869; dt William and Elizabeth Cox; m William T. Cammack 17 Nov 1889; d Marion 24 Jun 1900, bur Park Cem (6/28/00; 7/12/00))

CAMMACK, Mattie O. - recently helped organize the Matthews WCTU (11/10/98)

CAMMACK, Ward - age 9; s William T. and 'Emma' (Cox) (6/28/00; 7/12/00)

CAMMACK, William T. - m Emma Cox; Grant Co. Clerk (6/28/00)

CAREY, __ - see Mrs. C.J. HOWELL

CAREY, Charles - CW vet bur in BC Friends Cem (6/5/96)

CAREY, Ellen (Haisley) - dt Ira and Rebecca Haisley (9/10/97)

CAREY, Gervais - will speak at Fmt. Twp. Schs commencement June 11th (6/10/98)

CAREY, Gracie - mbr Oak Ridge WCTU (6/3/98)

CAREY, Ida - dt [John T.] Carey of NW of Fmt.; FFA student; d 22 May 1899 (5/25/99)

CAREY, Mary Lavina (Bogue) - b near Roseburg; age 36y, 9m, 14da; dt Thomas and Emily Bogue; m Joseph Henry Carey 22 Apr 1882; moved to KS ca 1888; had 6 children; d 10 Oct 1897, bur Park Cem (10/8/97; 10/15/97)

CAREY, Oliver A. - 26 Sep 1897 m Carrie A. Cragun of near Greentown (10/1/97)

CARPENTER, Emery - Chief, Fmt. Fire Company [i.e., Fire Dept.] (11/24/92)

CARPENTER, Henry - landholder advertising 'no hunting' on his property (10/13/92)

CARPENTER, Mary Jane - b Franklin Co. 25 Dec 1824; m 5 Apr 1846; widow; d 21 Jun 1891 (6/25/91)

CARROLL, Bert - to grad 9 Jun 1899 from Fmt. Twp. sch (6/1/99)

CARROLL, Delilah A. - see Delilah A. HOLLINGSWORTH

CARROLL, Mrs. Ella B. - 1st grade tchr, Fmt. Sch (11/12/91)

CARROLL, T.L. - is Fmt. plasterer and stone mason (6/20/89)

CARROLL, Will - 5 July 1889 shot Ed Clark at a sch bldg. near Jonesboro; Clark may not recover (7/18/89)

CARTER, __ - baby of M/M Robert Carter; d 27 Sep 1898 (9/29/98)

CARTER, Amanda M. - widow; of near Oak Ridge; d 28 Mar 1892 (4/7/92); lived 4 mi. NW of Fmt. in Liberty Twp. (4/14/92)

CARTER, Asa - and son are hired to take up slanting floor in Parker's Opera House and re-lay it on level (9/2/98); their work on floor is completed (9/29/98)

CARTER, George - b Surrey, NC 11 Feb 1816; s Solomon and Sarah; m 25 Nov 1836 Mary Buller; mbr U.B. Ch.; active in 'underground railroad'; lived on Deer Creek; d 10 Apr 1889 (4/11/89)

CARTER, Ida - 1891 grad, Liberty Twp. sch (5/21/91)

CARTER, Isaac - of [New] Cumberland; d 28 Mar 1899 (3/30/99)

CARTER, Mrs. Isaac - d recently (4/1/98)

CARTER, Isaac W. - of Liberty Twp.; age 60 (2/21/96)

CARTER, Jermina Jane - see Jermina Jane GRAY

CARTER, L.H. - mbr, Fmt. W.M. Ch. (4/16/97)

CARTER, Sally - see Edmund PETTIFORD

CASKEY, John H. - farmer living 3 mi. SE of Fmt.; moved there in 1871 (2/12/91); is injured when his horse ran away with him (7/2/97); Ind. Natural Gas & Oil Co. completes a fine gas well on his farm (9/20/00)

CASKEY, William J. - b Rush Co.; age 45; f Fmt. area sch tchr; brother of John Caskey; d at home of his father in Reno Co., KS 29 Mar 1898 (4/8/98;4/22/98)

CASSELL, Lew A. - attorney in Fmt. (4/14/92)

CASSELL, Mrs. Lew - is dt M/M Henry Winslow; and husband live in Swayzee (6/18/97)

CEMER, Charles - of Battle Creek, MI; will live with his brother, William Cemer, and att BC Sch (9/19/89)

CEMER, J.W. - att Battle Creek Coll, MI (12/25/90)

CHANCE, Ed - of Upland; while working with Oscar Felton at the Upland Zinc Smelting Works on 25 Feb 1899, Felton used a steel bar to cave in Chance's skull (3/2/99); he seems to be recovering (3/9/99)

CHARLES, Olive - see Dr. Olive WILSON

CHARLES, Albert S. - of Dallas Co., IA; brother of J.H. Charles; left Fmt. in 1871, is now visiting here (12/12/89)

CHARLES, Henry - clerk in Lucas Restaurant (5/3/00)

CHARLES, J.H. - is with Fairmount Mills (12/12/89)

CHARLES, Mattie - will be 1896-97 Fmt. Schs 4th grade tchr (3/6/96); 1899-1900 Fmt. Elementary Sch tchr (8/24/99)

CHARLES, Mildred - won 1st place in the WCTU silver medal speaking contest held at Bethel M.P. Ch. last Sunday (9/3/97); age ca 16 (2/8/00)

CHARLES, Rose - sister of J.H. Charles; never m; mbr Daughters of Rebecca; d 22 June 1889, bur Park Cem (6/27/89; 7/4/89)

CHASEY, Ol - is in 160th Ind. Regmt. In camp at Columbus, GA (1/12/99)

CHILDS, Charles - 10 of his sheep were killed by dogs 26 Nov 1897 (12/3/97)

CHURCHES
BACK CREEK (BC)FRIENDS - will host Quarterly Meeting next Sat. and Sun. with several ministers present (12/19/89); to host Northern Quarterly Meeting 17 Jan 1891 (1/15/91); Northern Quarterly Meeting will be moved to Fmt. Friends after new MH is constructed (3/26/91); Northern Quarterly Meeting Bible Sch Conference will be held here 18 Jul 1891 (7/2/91); Linais Haisley is a mbr (4/16/97)
BACK CREEK WESLEYAN METHODIST (BC W.M.) - Handley Broyles (dec) was a mbr (3/13/96); W.J. Neal is a mbr (4/16/97)
BETHEL METHODIST PROTESTANT (M.P.) - to be built on corner of Major Norton farm [SE corner of jct. of 800 S. and 400 E.] (2/11/92); to be built 0.5 mi. W of [Lake] Sch (3/17/92); MH is framed and sided (5/5/92); to be dedicated 1st Sun. in July (6/9/92); to be dedicated Sun. July 17; Rev. Benjamin Stout of WV to preach dedicatory sermon (6/30/92); D. Norris and Bert Pyles arrested for disturbing meeting on Sun. July 17th; they pilfered lunch baskets during meeting; Squire Frank Jones fined them $12.00 each and, in default of payment, jailed them at Marion (7/21/92); Prof. Overman organizes a singing class (9/1/92); will host Lake Sch and East Branch Sch for literary exercises on Thanksgiving Day (11/17/92); Fmt. Twp. Schs 1, 4, 6, and 7 took part in Thanksgiving Day exercises with Mrs. C. Duling as organist and C.M. Hobbs reading the scripture (12/1/92); pastor is M.F. Iliff (1/22/97); F.M. Haines is a mbr (4/16/97); WCTU silver medal speaking contest to be here Sun. afternoon (8/27/97); Mildred Charles won 1st place and Mary Winslow won 2nd place in the speaking contest last Sun. (9/3/97); Fmt. Twp. Schs commencement to be held here June 11th with Rev. Iliff giving the invocation (6/10/98); Georgia May Andrews is dec mbr (3/2/99)
CENTER CHRISTIAN - Jan 1890 new pastor will be Rev. Snodgrass (12/12/89); Rev. Eli Schmuck preached last Sat. and Sun. nights (1/22/91); M/M Will Goble are new mbrs (3/31/92); Rev. Briggs is no longer pastor (1/4/00)
DUNKARD CHURCH - is 3.5 mi. NE of Summitville (3/13/96)
EAST BRANCH FRIENDS - Ora Winslow is a mbr (4/16/97)
FAIRMOUNT BAPTIST/MISSIONARY BAPTIST - new MH foundation will soon be started (10/29/91); foundation being laid by El. Gossett and others (12/17/91); will cost $3,000 (1/7/92); MH to

CHURCHES (continued)
be built in spring (2/11/92); brick walls are up; roof to be slate (8/18/92); pastor is Lotus Aspy (3/27/96; 2/5/97); Retta Hall, mbr (4/16/97); Miss Flora Osborn (dec) was a mbr (1/26/99); Captolea Jennie (Bailey) Middleton (dec) was a mbr (2/23/99); T.W. Cox, pastor (5/11/99), now resigns to att Franklin Coll (9/13/00)
FAIRMOUNT CONGREGATIONAL - holds Sun. services in Scott's Opera House (12/27/88); Rev. C. Evans, pastor (2/7/89); Trustees are Levi Scott, W.B. Hollingsworth, Will Brown (2/10/89); bricks being laid for new MH (8/15/89); new MH being roofed (9/19/89); MH dedicated 15 Dec 1889; MH cost $5,750; Bldg. Committee included Dr. A. Henley, Levi Scott, William Lindsay; Rev. William Wiedenhoeft, pastor (12/19/89); Rev. S.W. Pollard, pastor (1/1/91); new pastor is Rev. Levi White (8/7/96); Allen Shuey is a mbr (4/16/97); Levi White resigns to be a pastor elsewhere (7/2/97); Rev. C.A. Riley is pastor (10/1/97); is electrically lighted by wires from LaRue's Light Plant (3/4/98); Belle Boyd, famous Confederate spy, lectured here 15 Mar 1899 (3/23/99); Eugene V. Debs, labor agitator, will give an address here 9 Apr 1899 (4/6/99); new pastor is Rev. F.B. Stearns of MI (1/25/00), and now resigns and goes back to MI (5/24/00)
FAIRMOUNT FRIENDS - Cyrus Hollingsworth drew up plans for new MH (3/19/91); Northern Quarterly to be moved here from BC after new MH is constructed (3/26/91); last meeting held in old MH yesterday, demolition of old MH begins today (5/21/91); foundation of new MH is started (7/2/91), is being laid (7/9/91); C.R. Small, SS Supt.; Frank Hammond, Asst. SS Supt. (7/9/91); brick laying started (9/24/91); bricks are laid to above MH windows (10/15/91); walls are up, ready for roof (11/5/91); Women's Foreign Missionary Society mbrs include Narcissa Nixon, Lizzie Peacock, Sarah Baldwin, Angie Pearson, Kate Hammonds, Elvira J. Small (11/26/91); MH is being plastered (12/10/91); large bell for new MH delivered, it weighs ca 1,300 lbs. (12/31/91); new seats are being installed in MH; Bldg. Committee mbrs are Nixon Winslow, Alpheus Henley, Cornelius Small, James M. Bell and John B. Seale; MH to be dedicated Sun. 21 Feb 1892 (2/11/92); new MH cost $8,900 (2/25/92); long-time mbr John Coahran has dec (10/6/92); pastor, Enos Harvey (1/29/97); Ryland Ratliff, mbr (4/16/97); Mrs. Mattie P. Wright, mbr and SS tchr (1/11/00)
FAIRMOUNT METHODIST EPISCOPAL (M.E.) - new MH to be dedicated (2/5/91), Sun. 15 Feb 1891 (2/5/91); new MH is 55' X 35' and

CHURCHES (continued)
cost $2,800 (2/26/91); Rev. J.F. Radcliffe/ Ratcliffe, pastor (3/12/91; 9/10/91); Mrs. Allie Nelson, mbr (11/5/91); new pastor, Rev. A. Greenman (5/19/92); Rev. Greenman resigns pastorate due to ill health (8/25/92); Charles H. Metts, pastor (9/1/92); J.W. Oborn, pastor; mbrs include Eva Hobbs and Margaret Life (1/3/96); H.M. Johnson, new pastor (4/10/96); pastor is D.I. Hower (4/9/97; 6/25/97); C.T. Parker is a mbr (4/16/97); new pastor is Rev. Millard Pell (5/4/99)
FAIRMOUNT METHODIST PROTESTANT (M.P.) - see Bethel M.P.
FAIRMOUNT ROMAN CATHOLIC - services were held 26 Feb 1889 in the residence of D.J. Riley; there is talk of starting a Ch. here (2/28/89); may be built next summer (2/11/92); ladies will hold a week-long bazaar in the old Parker Opera House starting Feb 15th (1/19/99); work starts on the new church bldg. on a lot in NE Fmt. near Big Four Glass Factory (5/10/00); bldg. framework is up (5/31/00)
FAIRMOUNT UNITED BRETHREN (U.B.)- Mary (Bird) Pickard (dec) was a mbr (8/24/99); pastor is Rev. Oxley (9/13/00)
FAIRMOUNT WESLEYAN METHODIST (W.M.) - Rev. Jacob Hester, pastor (2/7/89); Trustees are J.Tuttle and N.D. Cox (2/10/89); Rev. J.J. Coleman, pastor (6/25/91); J.F. Pressnall, pastor (1/22/97); L.H. Carter, mbr (4/16/97); D.F. Gordon, pastor (6/8/99); C.S. Smith, pastor (11/29/00)
FOWLERTON/LEACH UNITED BRETHREN - almost $300 has been pledged to build MH (3/5/97); foundation of MH is begun (4/16/97); to be dedicated 18 Jul 1897 (7/9/97)
GAS CITY BAPTIST - burned down 19 Feb 1896 (2/21/96)
GAS CITY WELSH - dedicated last Sun. PM (9/20/00)
HILL'S CHAPEL (African Methodist Episcopal = A.M.E.) - located in Weaver; mbrs and pastor will have a possum dinner on Christmas Day (12/24/91)
JONESBORO FRIENDS - Rev. Hiatt is holding a revival, several people claiming to be healed although Rev. Hiatt is not encouraging it (10/22/97); Miss Maude Millner of Leesburg, OH is the singer with Hiatt the evangelist (10/29/97)
JONESBORO METHODIST EPISCOPAL (M.E.) - Rev. J.W. McKaig, pastor (4/18/89); bldg. to be dedicated 8 Jul 1900 (6/28/00)
JONESBORO METHODIST PROTESTANT (M.P.) - Rev. M.F. Iliff, pastor (6/26/96)
JONESBORO 7TH DAY ADVENTIST - is being built (3/14/89)

CHURCHES (continued)
LEACH HOPEWELL - Fmt. Twp. Schs Commencement will be held here 2 Jun 1900 (5/24/00)
LINWOOD 'WHITE EGG' FRIENDS - George Collins and B.F. Albert contracted to build MH; Mrs. [Rev. Elmina B.] Harris holds services in White Egg Sch bldg. (3/12/91); SS is held in Sch bldg. (3/26/91); Rev. Con Shugart to hold Memorial Day service here (5/21/91); MH is nearing completion (7/23/91); located N of Hackleman; to be dedicated Sun.16 Aug 1891 (8/6/91; 8/13/91); was packed with people Sun. evening for a temperance lecture (10/1/91); referred to as 'Glenwood' by Fmt. News (12/3/91); Daisy Barr is holding a revival here (3/19/97)
LITTLE RIDGE FRIENDS - Rev. J.M. Wilbern preaches here each 2nd Sun. of each month (8/15/89); pastor is Stephen Scott (9/2/98)
OAK RIDGE FRIENDS - pastor, Micah Morris (1/26/99); Liberty Twp. Schs graduation to be held 17 Jun 1899 in MH (6/15/99)
PIKE UNITED BRETHREN (U.B.) - S of Fmt.; is having a revival (1/17/96); Ella Kester, mbr (4/16/97); may be called Fmt. U.B. (11/16/99)
PLEASANT GROVE [GRANT] M.P. - Z.C. Osborn, mbr (4/16/97); will meet 19 Feb 1898 to elect Trustees (1/28/98); Fmt. Twp. Schs graduation to be held here 9 Jun 1899 (6/1/99)
SALEM M.P. - in or near Liberty, Jefferson Twp.; Rev. Albright, pastor; L.P. Simons and J.O. Duling are mbrs (9/10/91); Levi Simons, mbr (4/16/97); is in Jefferson Twp.; will meet 10 Mar 1898 to elect Trustees (2/18/98); 4 mi. E of Fmt.; has been remodeled; will be dedicated Aug 14th (8/12/98); is in Fowlerton (8/19/98)
SOUTH MARION FRIENDS - MH, located 1 block W of Marion Normal Sch Bldg., was dedicated last Sun. (11/14/89)
UNION UNITED BRETHREN (U.B.) - M.M. Haines, mbr (4/16/97)

CIVIL WAR VETERANS - 130th Regmt. Ind. Vol. Inf. 8th annual reunion to be held Sep 8-9 at Fmt. Fair Grounds with a Camp Fire program in Scott's Opera House on evening of Sep 8 (8/18/92); local 130th Regmt. vets att reunion include: Samuel Bowers of Cadiz; George N. Allred and H.M. McCaski of Rigdon; John Gibson of Jonesboro; and W.B. Hollingsworth, H. Gardner, E.L. Payne, William Smith, B.S. Payne and E.H. Alexander of Fmt. (9/15/92); Fmt. area vets of Co. K, 130th Ind. Inf. att reunion in Elwood on 6 Aug 1896 included: Will Smith, Bailey Payne, George Allred, Caleb Moon, Henry Gardner, W.B. Hollingsworth, E.L. Payne and Asbury Starr;

local vets from other units att include J.B. Smithson, Elijah Alexander, Capt. Weston, J.B. Smith and Marion Wood (8/7/96); local CW vets of Co. H, 12th Ind. Regmt. Include: of Fmt. - Foster Davis, John B. Hollingsworth, Frank Jones, Rust Kelsay, Alex Little, George W. Thorn; of Gas City - William P. Roush; of Jonesboro - Henry Clapper (1/12/99)

CLAPPER, Henry - CW vet of Jonesboro; wife invited CW Co. H vets as a surprise for his 72nd birthday 6 Jan 1899 (1/12/99)

CLARK, Ed - 5 July 1889 was shot by Will Carroll at a sch house near Jonesboro, may not recover (7/18/89)

CLARK, F.J. - age 78; of Jonesboro; was bur 23 Jan 1889 (1/24/89)

CLARK, Millard - hunted rabbits with Gib LaRue and Bob Ray last Fri. (12/5/89); Engineer for Fmt. Water & Light Station (10/26/99)

CLARK, Raymond W. - b 2 Oct 1894; s Morton W. and Lucy Jane Clark; d 9 Aug 1897 (8/20/97)

CLODFELTER, Noah J. - says he will cause the I.A. & M. Railway to be built from Marion to Anderson by way of Fmt. and Jonesboro (5/8/96); is ill in Indianapolis (2/5/97); is physically and mentally ill; is patient in Central Insane Hospital, Indianapolis (5/24/00)

CLOTHIER, George - Corp, Co. A., 160th Ind. Regmt.; is home on leave (2/23/99)

CLOUD, Rachel - see Stephen SCOTT

COAHRAN, John - d Fmt. 19 Sep 1892 (9/22/92); b Delaware 23 Dec 1807; f mbr Baptists; mbr Friends; bur Park Cem (10/6/92)

COGGESHALL, Bertha May - see Bertha May JOHNSON

COGGESHALL, Eli - lives 1 mi. S of Marion Normal Coll (8/12/98)

COILE, Edith - see George HESTER/[HERTER]

COLEMAN, George - Dillon Glass Works employee (7/2/91)

COLEMAN, J.J. - Fmt. W.M. Ch. pastor (6/25/91)

COLEMAN, Margaret A. (O'Brien) - lived in Fmt.; b 26 May 1860; m Daniel Coleman 7 May 1879; mbr W.M. Ch.; d 27 May 1892, bur Park Cem (6/2/92)

COLES [STATION] - is on C.I.&E. RR between Fmt. and Swayzee; 21 Apr 1900 at Grand Opening of William Comer's General Store, a drunken Albert Silvers shot and wounded Al Glessner in the forehead (4/26/00)

COLLINS, Albert - Center Sch tchr 1892-93 (9/1/92)

COLLINS, George - and B.F. Albert contracted to build White Egg Friends MH (3/12/91)

COMER, J.M. - of near Hackleman; given party for his 39th birthday 27 Aug 1900 (8/30/00)

COMER, William - had the Grand Opening of his new General Store in Coles [Station] 21 Apr 1900 (4/26/00)

COMPTON, Albert - contracted to dig the Kelsay Branch of Galatia Creek Ditch near Lake Galatia for $925 (2/1/00)

CONE, Charles - Fmt. soldier serving in Philippines (9/21/99)

CONE, Jack - is a Fmt. blacksmith (2/19/91); blacksmith for Dillon Glass Works (4/23/91)

CONE, Vint - is engineer for Fmt. Mills while engineer Zep Gossett is ill (10/29/91)

CONNER, Mrs. __ - of Phlox; will have charge of FFA dormitory 1898-99 (8/26/98)

CONNER, W.B. - started Conner Drug Store ca 1889 (4/14/92)

COOK, __ - s M/M Jason Cook of Hackleman area; d recently (4/22/98)

COOPER, Bessie (Busing) - sister of J.R. Busing (6/28/00)

COOPER, Hattie - mbr Fmt. Women's Relief Corps (11/14/89)

COOPER, Hiram - owns livery stable started ca 1888 (4/14/92)

COOPER, Roll - 15 Sep 1897 m Bessie Busing (9/17/97); Big Four Window Glass Co. employee (1/4/00)

COPPOCK, Calvin - age 73; of Jonesboro; d 11 Sep 1898 (9/15/98)

COPPOCK, John - of Jonesboro; age 86; d 15 Jan 1891 (1/22/91)

COPPOCK, Martha E. - sues Eben E. Coppock for divorce (4/20/99)

COPPOCK, Nora - see Nora HAWORTH

COPPOCK, Ursula - see Ursula JOHNSON

CORDER, Robert - of Jonesboro; recently dec; bur Park Cem (8/12/98)

CORN, __ - baby of William Corn of near Leachburg d 30 Dec 1890 (1/1/91)

CORN, Mrs. Joe - of 3 mi. E of Fmt.; dt Ransom Ice (8/31/99)

CORN, Joseph T. - landholder advertising 'no hunting' on his property (10/13/92)

CORN, Mattie - see Wilson SIMONS

COUNCIL, Roll - has a Fowlerton blacksmith shop (3/12/97; 4/16/97)

COWGILL, Josie - is Earlham Coll student (4/2/97)

COWGILL, Miss Louie - att Earlham Coll (9/10/91)

COWGILL, Luzena F. - see Harry O. WHITNEY

COWGILL, Macy - is Earlham Coll student (9/10/91)

COWGILL, Mollie (Norton) - of Jonesboro is dt Major B.V. Norton (1/28/98)

COWGILL, Samuel C. - has a large tile factory at Summitville (1/25/00); is touring the Mediterranean and the Holy Land with Elwood O. Ellis (4/19/00); left E.O. Ellis and sailed home from Liverpool yesterday because of the failing health of his son-in-law Harry Whitney (5/17/00)

COWGILL, Mrs. Samuel C. - of near Summitville; m; mbr Fmt. Friends; d 15 Jul 1899, bur Park Cem (7/20/99)

COX, __ - see Mrs. Johny SEALE

COX, Ann Marie - see Thomas H. LAWRENCE

COX, Burl W. - mbr Co. A, 160th Ind. Regmt. (12/1/98); in camp at Columbus, GA (1/12/99); is employee of Alexandria Axe Co. (1/18/00); is in poor health; is granted US pension of $12 per month (11/29/00)

COX, Cora - see Clinton HAISLEY

COX, Estella (Smith) - dt Rev. Albert Smith; m Martin E. Cox 22 Mar 1896; will live in Fmt. (3/27/96)

COX, Hannah - see J.C. JESSUP

COX, Hannah Jane - see Hannah Jane PAYNE

COX, John W. - lives 0.75 mi. W of Fmt. where he sells apple tree nursery stock (3/24/92); has 2-yr old grape vines and young fruit trees for sale (4/17/96); left for KS this wk to help thresh wheat (6/28/00)

COX, Mrs. John - last wk, an arm was broken by a cow she was milking (8/9/00)

COX, Malinda - see Joseph RICH

COX, Margaret Emler 'Emma' - see Margaret CAMMACK

COX, Mrs. Milton - of W of Fmt. is dt Robert P. and Rachel C. (Vestal) Petty (both dec) (5/17/00)

COX, N.D. - Trustee, Fmt. W.M. Ch. (2/10/89)

COX, N.S., DDS - grad Ohio Coll of Dental Surgery, Cincinnati; recently set up his dental office in the Bank Blk. (4/14/92); Fmt. dentist (5/22/96); s Alfred Cox of Anderson (10/8/97); and wife move to Greenfield after selling his practice to Dr. Will N. Ratliff (3/11/98)

COX, Nathan D. - Park Cem caretaker (8/27/91; 1/5/99)

COX, Nora - see Nora GREGG

COX, Seth - and Micah Baldwin have a Fmt. Shoe Shop (10/15/91); Chief, Fmt. Volunteer Fire Dept. (4/14/92)

COX, T.W. - Fmt. Baptist Ch. pastor (5/11/99); resigns pastorate to att Franklin Coll (9/13/00)

COX, Thomas - CW vet bur in unmarked grave in BC Friends Cem (5/23/89; 6/5/96)

COYLE, Mamie - age 16; dt M/M John Coyle; d 8 Aug 1898 (8/12/98)

CRABB, O. - mbr/officer, Fmt. IOOF (1/4/00)

CRAGUN, CARRIE A. - see Oliver A. CAREY

CRAWFORD, Cyrus - CW pension is increased to $12 per month (9/24/91)

CRILLEY, Miss Grace Maxine - will take the position of operator with the Fmt. Telephone Co. (4/12/00); grad Fmt. HS 1900 (5/10/00)

CRISCO, Perry - s Winfield Crisco; d 12 Mar 1889 (3/14/89)

CRISCO, Mrs. Winfield - lives 2 mi. E of Fmt.; grand-dt of Nathan Little (12/22/98)

CROW, Jack - recently discharged from Co. A, 160th Ind. Regmt. (12/29/98)

CROW, Margaret - of near Matthews; f of Fmt.; widow of Michael Crow; d 17 May 1900 (5/17/00)

CROWELL, Emma - b Fmt. 16 Apr 1874; dt M/M Milton Crowell; d 1 Nov 1889, bur BC Friends Cem (11/7/89)

CROWELL, Milton - b Randolph Co., NC 9 Sept 1838; m; CW vet; mbr GAR; mbr Friends; d 12 Apr 1891 (4/16/91), bur Park Cem (6/5/96)

CRULL, Henry - of Matthews fell dead in his carriage this wk (9/10/97)

CURRIE, Gabriel - owns brood and sale stable; has 5 draft horses at stud (4/14/92)

CURRIE, Mrs. Gabe - m; dt Mrs. Fred Stine (1/31/89)

CURTIS, J.W. - officer, Beeson Post, GAR (12/10/91)

DALE, infant - child of M/M J.W. Dale; d 18 Aug 1898, bur Park Cem (8/26/98)

DALE, Dr. George - recently setup dental office in Fmt. (2/7/89); is divorcing his wife, Emma J. Dale (9/12/89); Fmt. dental surgeon (4/14/92)

DALE, Hal - enlisted in regular army; is enroute to Philippines (6/7/00); s J.W. Dale; is in 6th Cav. fighting in China (9/20/00)

DALE, J.W. - owns/operates Dale Hardware (3/11/98)

DALRYMPLE, __ - infant of M/M Charles Dalrymple of Fmt.; d 21 Jun 1899 (6/22/99)

DANIEL, James W. - of near New Cumberland; age 75y, 1m, 19da; m; d 7 Mar 1892 (3/17/92)

DANIELS, Mrs. Will - of Muncie; dt M/M Robert Hasting (7/10/96)

DAUGHERTY, Charles - a Summitville druggist (1/14/98)

DAUGHERTY, Mrs. Charles - of Summitville; dt T.D. and Clara (dec) Myers of Fmt. (12/31/97)

DAUGHERTY, Elam - of near Oak Ridge; m; age 71; d 2 Feb 1892, bur Park Cem (2/4/92)

DAUGHERTY, Mrs. Etta - Little Ridge WCTU president (6/3/98)

DAUSE, Lizzie (Dillon) - b Madison Co. 6 May 1837; dt Jesse and Mary Dillon (both dec); Sep 1852 m Micajah Winslow; lived in Jonesboro area for several yr then in KS where Micajah d 3 Sep 1875; m 2nd 1 Aug 1896 Edward Dause; moved to New Holland, Wabash Co.; d 27 Mar 1897 (4/9/97)

DAVIDSON, Angie Mary - b 12 May 1900; dt Nathan and Elizabeth E.; d 1 Jul 1900 (7/12/00)

DAVIDSON, Sebborn - of Oak Ridge area; s Nathan Davidson (11/3/98)

DAVIS, Cyrus - lives 2 mi. E of Fmt. (2/19/91)

DAVIS, David - of near Fmt.; s John J. and Margaret (Breckenridge) Davis (both dec) (11/16/99)

DAVIS, David D. - mbr/officer, Fmt. IOOF (1/4/00); mbr Fmt. K. of P. Lodge (1/25/00)

DAVIS, Effie - mbr Fmt. Women's Relief Corps (11/14/89)

DAVIS, Elwood - and T.J. Lucas own/operate the f C.R. Small Hardware (4/14/92)

DAVIS, Foster - b Grant Co.; attorney in Grant Co. since 1875 (4/14/92); wife is Dorinda (8/18/92); CW vet of Co. H, 12th Ind. Regmt.; att party with other Co. H mbrs 6 Jan 1899 (1/12/99)

DAVIS, Frank - is Supt., Citizen's Gas Co. replacing Fred Macy (1/4/00)

DAVIS, Fred - baker for Lucas Restaurant; 2 Feb 1899 m Perna Overman, dt R.E. Overman (3/30/99)

DAVIS, Henry - a Fmt. veterinary surgeon (5/2/89; 4/14/92)

DAVIS, John - works for J.H. Wilson in the BeeHive (7/25/89)

DAVIS, John - landowner near Fmt. advertising that he permits no hunting on his property (11/12/97)

DAVIS, John R. 'Ruff' - 27 Oct 1889 m Mossie Hasting (10/31/89); d 20 Jun 1899 (6/22/99)

DAVIS, John W. - is embalmer; owns Fmt. furniture store; 16 Nov 1898 m Laura Robison, dt M/M W. Robison of near Walton (11/24/98); mbr of Fmt. Gun Club (9/21/99); a winner in Gun Club shoot held last Sat. (11/1/00)

DAVIS, Joseph M. - is Earlham Coll student (9/14/99)

DAVIS, Margaret (Breckinridge) - b 11 Sep 1828; at Ogden 5 Aug 1848 m John J. Davis (dec in Tipton Co.); mbr Christian Ch.; d near Fmt. 4 Nov 1899 (11/16/99)

DAVIS, Matt - employee of a stave factory in N. Fmt. (11/29/00)

DAVIS, Mattie - mbr Fmt. Women's Relief Corps (11/14/89); b 5 Sep 1871; dt Foster and Dorinda Davis; mbr W.M. Ch.; d 7 Aug 1892, bur Park Cem (8/11/92; 8/18/92)

DAVIS, Nancy - see Nancy MILLIKAN

DAVIS, Ozzie D. - b 16 Sep 1890; s John R. and Mosaline (Hasting) Davis; lived 1 mi. S of Fmt.; d 19 Mar 1897, bur Park Cem (3/19/97; 4/2/97)

DAVIS, Verling W. - is BC Sch tchr (8/31/99); of Fmt.; s Foster Davis (10/18/00)

DAVIS, Mrs. Will - of Liberty Twp.; d 24 Oct 1892 (10/27/92)

DEAN, __ - 18 month old child of Job Dean; d 2 Mar 1889, bur BC Friends Cem (3/7/89)

DEAN, __ - b 26 Jan 1897; dt M/M Calvin Dean (2/5/97)

DEAN, __ - b 17 Feb 1897; dt M/M Glenn Dean (3/5/97)

DEAN, Cal - of S of Fmt.; barn burned Tuesday killing his Clydesdale stallion (5/21/91); is a Fmt. auctioneer (4/30/97)

DEAN, Ella - see Ella DULING

DEAN, Hamilton - a Fmt. Attorney-at-Law (5/16/89); s William G. Dean (dec) of Owen Co. (6/11/91)

DEAN, Harrison 'Harry' - CW vet bur BC Friends Cem (5/23/89; 6/5/96)

DEAN, J.H. - tchr, Leachburg Sch (12/5/89); s William G. Dean of Owen Co. (4/23/91)

DEAN, Miss Nellie - is Marion Coll student (1/12/99)

DEAN, William G. - of Owen Co.; d 19 Apr 1891 (4/23/91)

DEANER, J.W. - sells Columbia Hotel to W. Welty (11/19/97)

DEBS, Eugene B. - labor agitator; will give address Sun. 9 Apr 1899 in Fmt. Congregational Ch. (4/6/99)

DeCOURSEY, William - age 27; m; of Sims; d 20 Nov 1898 as result of gas well drilling accident near Rubber Works in Jonesboro (11/24/98)

DEEREN, Naomi L. - landholder advertising 'no hunting' on her property (10/13/92)

DEERING, Alex - officer, Beeson GAR Post (12/10/91); of 1 mi. N, 5 mi. E of Fmt.; m; age 50; d recently, bur New Cumberland Cem (7/10/96)

DELEAMP, Minnie (Baldwin) - of Goshen; dt M/M Micah Baldwin (2/21/89)

DeLONG, Josie - m 1st Laban Andrews (d ca 1888); m 2nd John DeLong (3/2/99)

DEMICK, Hugh - is blacksmith in Radley (1/18/00)

DENNIS, Mrs. John - is dt Nickolas Keener (dec) of Winchester (7/16/97)

DeSELMS, [Abigail] (Brookshire) - of Anderson; sister of Luther and Thomas Brookshire; d 14 Apr 1889 (4/18/89)

DeSHON, __ - b 23 Apr 1891; s M/M James Deshon (4/30/91)

DeSHON, Frank - volunteered for army in response to Spanish-American War (4/29/98); is in 160th Ind. Regmt. In camp at Columbus, GA (1/12/99)

DeSHON, Lizzie L. - mbr Fmt. Women's Relief Corps (11/14/89)

DeSHON, Pheba E. - mbr Fmt. Women's Relief Corps (11/14/89)

DICKERSON, Alvin - 1891-92 tchr, Jefferson Twp. Sch. #10 (3/31/92)

DICKEY, Anna M. (Mason) - b Grant Co. 28 Feb 1867; dt George (dec 29 June 1886) and __ (dec 3 Jan 1885) Mason of Hackleman area; m Prof. J. Marcus Dickey ca Aug 1887; d 2 Sept 1889, bur Marion IOOF Cem (9/5/89; 9/12/89)

DICKEY, Homer - BC Sch tchr (4/2/91); to teach in Fmt. Public Schs this fall (9/3/91)

DICKEY, John Marcus - b Fayette Co. ca 1859; att Spiceland and Tipton Normals; taught 4 terms in Liberty Twp; att State Normal 2 yr; taught in Fmt. Sch 1 yr; after further study in Boston, MA is now on FFA faculty; fall 1887 m his f student, Anna Mason (dec); mbr Christian Ch.; born a Democrat, reared a Republican, is now an extreme Prohibitionist (10/24/89)

DICKEY, Hugh - of SW of Fmt.; host to James Whitcomb Riley who is visiting in Dickey's home; brought his guest to Fmt. recently (8/23/00)

DICKEY, Lem - last Sun. in Liberty Twp. m Gertrude, dt Isaac Hollowell (3/31/92)

DICKEY, Marcus - mgr. for James Whitcomb Riley (8/23/00)

DICKEY, O. Frank - BC Sch tchr (10/8/91; 12/17/91)

DICKINSON, H.W. - operates a Fmt. meat market he purchased from Newt Allen (4/19/00)

DILLIE, Josiah - purchased S fraction of Sec. 12 on 10 Jun 1829 (1/7/92)

DILLON, __ - b 24 Mar 1891; s M/M Arthur Dillon (3/26/91)

DILLON, Allen - came to Fmt. area in 1840; started Dillon Glass Works; is selling 138 Fmt. bldg. lots in Dillon Addition (4/14/92); lived just N of Fmt.; b Clinton Co., OH 13 Mar 1836; s Richard and Elizabeth Dillon; was a gunsmith; m Kesiah Henley 17 Apr 1857; mbr Friends; d 3 Jan 1899, bur Park Cem (1/5/99; 1/12/99)

DILLON, Clara - see Ed SIEGEL

DILLON, Claude - 3 Apr 1898 m Minnie Nelson, will live in Fmt. (4/8/98)

DILLON, Jesse - owns/operates Dillon's Restaurant (7/25/89)

DILLON, Mrs. Jesse - mother of Frank Swope of Marion (2/19/91)

DILLON, Keziah (Henley) - dt Phineas and Mary Henley; 17 Apr 1857 m Allen Dillon (1/12/99)

DILLON, Lizzie - see Lizzie DAUSE

DILLON, Richard - s Allen and Keziah (Henley) Dillon (1/5/99)

DILLON, Samuel - lived in Fmt. area; s Richard and Elizabeth Dillon; brother of Allen Dillon (1/12/99)

DOBSON, Harry Lindsey - b 14 Feb 1896; s John F. and Lizzie E.; d 2 Mar 1897 (3/5/97)

DOHERTY, Miss Cora - teachs in Little Ridge Sch as assistant to Ancil Ratliff (12/5/89)

DOUGLAS, __ - see Mrs. John NOSE

DOUGLAS, Joseph - serv Co. H, 8th Ind. Inf. during CW; d 4 Mar 1899, bur Jonesboro cem (3/9/99)

DOWNS, Frank - mbr of Fmt. Gun Club (9/21/99)

DOYLE, John - mbr of Fmt. Gun Club (9/21/99)

DRAPER, Margaret - see Joseph RICH

DRIGGS, Asa A. - mbr of Fmt. Gun Club (9/21/99); s Asa L.; Fmt. hardware merchant (3/15/00)

DRIGGS, Asa L. - b Alleghany Co., PA 14 Feb 1815; m 1st 1835 Mary Miservey (dec); in 1865 m 2nd Sarah E. Rose (d 28 Aug 1889); lived Fmt. with s, Asa; d 9 Mar 1900, bur Fayetteville cem, Fayette Co. (3/15/00)

DROOK, David - crew foreman on Clodfelter RR construction site N of Summitville; a disgruntled workman, Jim Stanley, struck Drook with a rock; Drook is expected to recover (6/25/97)

DRUCKMILLER, Melvin - mbr Fmt. Friends boy's SS class (1/11/00)

DULING, __ - see Mrs. Charles M. HOBBS

DULING, Blanche - will grad 9 Jun 1899 from Fmt. Twp. Schs (6/1/99)

DULING, Mrs. C. - was organist for literary exercises for Fmt. Twp. Schs 1,4,6, and 7 held Thanksgiving Day in Bethel P.M. MH (12/1/92)

DULING, Edmond - landholder advertising 'no hunting' on his property (10/13/92)

DULING, Ella (Dean) - dt William Dean (dec) of Owen Co.; m Thomas Duling (4/16/91; 4/23/91)

DULING, Emma - dt of Thomas Duling; is given party for her 12th birthday on 23 May 1892 (5/26/92)

DULING, J.O. - mbr of Salem Ch. (9/10/91)

DULING, John - landholder advertising 'no hunting' on his property (10/13/92)

DULING, Syna M. - see T.P. LATHAM

DULING, Thomas Dean, Sr. - b Hampshire Co., VA 22 Nov 1811; m 4 Feb 1836 Nancy Meskimen; mbr M.P. Ch.; d 4 Jan 1891 (1/8/91)

DULING, Mrs. Thomas - of 3.5 mi. E of Fmt.; d 25 Dec 1900 (12/27/00)

DUNCAN, Annie (Moon) - m John W. Duncan 25 Apr 1889; d 14 May 1891 at her home SW of Fmt., bur BC Friends Cem (5/21/91)

DUNCAN, John W. - 25 Apr 1889 m Annie Moon of Little Ridge area (5/2/89)

DUNLAP, Alonzo - leaves for KS to help thresh wheat (6/28/00)

DUNN, Marietta - secretary, Matthews WCTU (11/10/98)

DUNN, T.J. - age 44; m; of New Cumberland; d 11 Apr 1899 (4/13/99)

DYE, W.D. - left for KS this wk to help thresh wheat (6/28/00)

DYSON, Thomas - of Little Ridge; and wife celebrated their 5th wedding anniv 2 Apr 1897 (4/9/97)

EASTER, Lucinda A. - see Austin P. WARD

EASTES, __ - b 14 Sept 1889; s M/M Charles E. Eastes (9/19/89)

EASTES, Charles E. - s Lemuel F. Eastes of New Corner; has a Fmt. harness shop (5/16/89); sells carriages, buggies and carts (8/8/89)

EASTES, Mrs. Charles E. - dt H.M. Mallow of Warren (11/7/89)

EASTES/ESTES, James - Fmt. soldier serving in Philippines (9/21/99)

EASTES, Mrs. Will - d at Leach 19 Feb 1898, bur Park Cem (2/25/98)

EATON, Mary - mbr Oak Ridge WCTU (6/3/98)

EATON, Mrs. Ot - of Hackleman area is dt M/M __ Wright of near Normal (3/30/99)

EATON, Porter - baby of M/M Ot Eaton of Hackleman area (10/19/99)

EATON, Thomas B. - of Fmt.; age ca 69; d 8 Mar 1889, bur Vinson Cem (3/14/89)

ECCLES, Iliff A. - b near Matthews; age 15m, 16da; s Jesse and Elesta Eccles; d Fmt. 16 Aug 1899, bur Matthews Cem (8/24/99)

EDWARDS, __ - b 12 Feb 1889; dt M/M O.W. Edwards (2/10/89)

EDWARDS, Henry - age 86 (3/22/00); b NC 27 Apr 1814; moved to Wayne Co. ca 1820; ca 1835 m Thirza S. Ellis (dec 1887); mbr M.E. Ch.; d 25 Aug 1900 (8/30/00)

EDWARDS, Nathan W. - owns/operates Edwards Drug Store (7/25/89; 1/31/96); established his drug store ca 1878

(4/14/92); s Henry Edwards (8/27/97); is re-elected to Fmt. Sch Board (6/15/99)

EDWARDS, Orv W. - Edwards Drug Store employee; brother of N.W. Edwards (7/25/89; 4/14/92)

EDWARDS, Xenophon - 6 Feb 1897 is given party for his 17th birthday (2/12/97); DePauw Univ student (9/24/97; 1/5/99); 1899-1900 Fmt. HS tchr (8/24/99)

ELLIOTT, __ - see Mrs. Oren GIBSON

ELLIOTT, __ - b 22 Oct 1899; s M/M Anson Elliott (10/26/99)

ELLIOTT, Mrs. Ed - of El Morro; dt M/M William Moon, now living in FL (12/22/98)

ELLIOTT, Henry - lived near North Grove; d ca 21 Feb 1897, bur BC Friends Cem (2/19/97)

ELLIOTT, Isaac - taught sch ca 1870 (10/17/89)

ELLIOTT, John M. - of Howard Co.; m; d 4 Apr 1900 while visiting in Fmt. (4/5/00)

ELLIOTT, Mahala C. - see Mahala C. (Humbard) ARNETT

ELLIOTT, Ransom Franklin - b 22 Nov 1897; s Stanley P. and Louie B. Elliott; d 14 Dec 1897 (12/24/97)

ELLIOTT, Ruth - in 1893 was a stockholder in Farmers & Merchants Bank (2/22/00)

ELLIOTT, William S. - a new town on his Liberty Twp. farm on C.I.&E. RR may be named El Morro (9/15/98)

ELLIS, __ - see Dr. S.M. NOLDER

ELLIS, Cressie - dt Rev./M E.O. Ellis of Richmond (12/1/98)

ELLIS, Rev. Elwood O. - taught sch in Fmt. 1884-85 (10/17/89); Grant Co. Supt. of Schs (3/19/91); s James M. and Louisa (Moon)

Ellis (7/16/91); f Co. Supt. of Schs; is new Principal, FFA (9/17/91); is Clerk, Ind. Yearly Meeting of Friends (10/8/91); Principal, Fmt. HS (4/14/92); resigned as recorded Friends Minister to devote full time to being FFA Supt./tchr (5/1/96); lives in Richmond where he is pastor of S. 8th St. Friends Ch. (7/15/98); is touring the Mediterranean and the Holy Land with Samuel C. Cowgill (4/19/00); returned from Europe (6/21/00)

ELLIS, Hannah - is in charge of FFA dormatory (9/3/91)

ELLIS, Louisa (Moon) - b Clinton Co., OH 20 Jul 1825; dt Daniel H. and Rachel Moon; m James M. Ellis 23 Jul 1845; mbr Friends, is an Elder; d 12 Jul 1891, bur Harrisburg Cem (7/16/91)

ELLIS, Mamie - of Oak Ridge; FFA freshman (9/22/98)

ELLIS, Myrtle - dt James Ellis (9/3/91)

ELLIS, Thirza S. - see Henry EDWARDS

EL MORRO - a new grain elevator is being built here (12/29/98); - see RADLEY

EVANS, Rev. C. - pastor, Fmt. Congregational Ch. (2/7/89)

EVANS, Fountain - age ca 88; b NC; lived in Fmt.; d last Sunday, bur Weaver Cem; colored (3/30/99)

EVERGREEN CEMETERY - will be in charge of Robert L. Wilson in the absence of D. Walthall (2/7/89); is adjacent to BC Friends Cem; Ezra Walthall of Jonesboro is advertising lots for sale (9/7/99)

EWING, W.M. - left for KS last wk to help thresh wheat (6/28/00)

FAIRMOUNT, Town of - C.W. & M. Railroad, completed through Fmt. in summer of 1874 (1/7/92); Main St. is being graveled (10/24/89); Fmt. Health Officer is Dr. J.O. Lowman (5/14/91); during past 2 yr sidewalks in business district along Main and Washington Streets were bricked/stoned (1/7/92); Volunteer Fire Dept. Chief is Seth Cox; has 30 firemen, a hand engine, and 600 feet of hose (4/14/92); a fire 1 Oct 1892 burned several business' with a loss of $20,000 (10/6/92); a petition to establish a Fmt. Water

FAIRMOUNT (continued)
Works is being pursued (11/24/92); E. Smith, Town Clerk
(6/25/97); at least 7 fire alarm boxes are installed in various
parts of Fmt.; Riley Jay is Marshall; Esom O. Leach, Deputy Marshall
(6/5/96); Big Four RR sends 6 passenger trains through town
daily, 3 going N and 3 going S (6/19/96); 6 gas wells in town
(2/5/97); 5 Oct 1897 Town Board granted franchise for electric
plant to William H. Lindsey; E. Smith is Supt., Water Works
(10/8/97); Town Board granted franchise to Gilbert LaRue to
construct an electric light plant (11/12/97); M.A. Hiatt, Town
Board Pres. (12/3/97); Town Board buys 2-horse fire wagon to
carry hoses and ladders (3/11/98); town has no saloon (3/25/98);
electric light plant of Gilbert LaRue is purchased/ leased by town
(12/1/98); Barney O'Riley is first prisoner in new jail
(3/9/99); Jap Wilson is Deputy Postmaster (3/30/99); electric
street lights were 1st used Sat. night 22 Apr 1899 (4/27/99);
town accepts LaRue Light Plant (6/15/99); hires William Bowers
as electrician for $45 per month (6/22/99); Millard Clark is
Water & Light Station engineer (10/19/99); G.A. Fletcher, Town
Clerk (1/18/00); rural free delivery of mail is approved for Fmt.
Route No. 1, which will be ca 25 mi. in length (3/8/00); rural free
delivery will cause closing of Weaver Post Office (3/22/00); Austin
Harvey delivers mail on Rural Route No. 1 (3/29/00); 2 Apr 1900
rural mail delivery began (4/5/00); James Whitcomb Riley is
guest of Hugh Dickey of SW of Fmt.; Hugh brought Riley to Fmt. in his
buggy and several people visited with Riley (8/23/00); Gov.
Theodore Roosevelt came to Fmt. by rail at 8:50, spoke to 4,000
people for 10 minutes asking them to re-elect President McKinley
(10/11/00); Main St. to be bricked from 8th St. to Henley Ave. as
will Henley Ave. S to Taylor St. (12/10/00)
AMERICAN WINDOW GLASS FACTORY - Philip Matter is on Board of
Directors (10/25/00)
BAKERY & RESTAURANT - prop., F.A. Bullinger (7/23/91;
4/14/92)
BALDWIN & COX - are boot and shoe repairers (10/22/91;
4/14/92)
BARBERSHOP & BATH ROOM - sold by Riley Jay to Marion Tweedy
(10/17/89); sold by Riley Jay to Daniel W. Gallimore
(11/12/91), who has added a bath room (4/14/92)
BEAL SHOE SHOP - owned/operated by Jacob Beals; moved to bldg.
across street N of Flanagan's Store (3/4/98)

41

FAIRMOUNT (continued)
BEASLEY DRUG STORE - owned/operated by Will Beasley (7/25/89); sells drugs, books, stationary, wallpaper and paint (7/2/91)
BEEHIVE GROCERY & DRY GOODS - owned/operated by J.H. Wilson (7/25/89; 6/4/91), who started it ca 1881 (4/14/92); Will E. Wilson resigns, purchases Latham's Vehicle & Harness Manufacturing (4/8/98)
BEESON GROCERY STORE - owned by A. Beeson (3/27/96)
BELL WINDOW GLASS FACTORY - is in operation (11/17/98); John Borrey, mgr. (12/1/98); F.B. Wilkinson, office mgr., resigns and Edward Welsh, bookkeeper, is promoted to office mgr. (6/28/00); John Borrey resigns as mgr. (11/15/00); Frank Andrick, Asst. Supt. (11/29/00)
BIG FOUR BARBERSHOP - M.M. Snodgrass, prop. has installed a bath in his shop (3/8/00)
BIG FOUR RESTAURANT - owned/managed by Perry Wood (2/8/00); purchased by Isaac Lemon (6/7/00)
BIG FOUR WINDOW GLASS WORKS - Frank Riddle is an employee (5/22/96); Elmer Hiatt, night watchman (7/9/97); is operating (11/17/98); employees include Roll Cooper (1/4/00), Ed Robinson (1/18/00), Will Glover as blacksmith (8/23/00); mgr. is A.L. Reed (8/30/00)
BLACKSMITH SHOP - owned/operated by J.J. Brown (4/14/92)
BLACKSMITH SHOP - owned/operated by Samuel Fritch and W.E. Gossett (4/14/92)
BORREY BLOCK - newly built; is being wired by electrician Will Bowers (9/20/00)
BORREY WINDOW GLASS FACTORY - being built on site of old Wood & Sluder Sawmill by partners J. Borrey, George Hetley and F.B. Wilkinson; foundation is being laid (4/29/98)
BOWLING ALLEY - is opened adjacent to Parker's Opera House (4/15/98); W.W. Paddock has sold his interest to E.E. Briles (12/21/99); placed in Beasley Bldg. in 1898; is now removed due to lack of customers (6/14/00)
BRILES SAWMILL - located 3.5 mi. SW of Fmt.; owned/operated by Jacob Briles; employs 6 to 20 men (4/14/92)
BRILES & LAWRENCE DRESSMAKING SHOP - on Penn St.; operated by Mrs. Jacob Briles and her sister, India Lawrence (8/24/99)
BRUSH & POGUE ELECTRICAL SUPPLY HOUSE - owned/operated by G.A. Brush & W.M. Pogue (4/14/92)

FAIRMOUNT (continued)
A.D. BRYAN & BRO. HARDWARE/IMPLEMENT STORE - owned/ operated by Bryan brothers (7/25/89); established ca 1876; sells John Deere plows (4/14/92)
W.H. CAMPBELL- employes 20-30 men; deals in heading, piling and saw timber (1/7/92)
CENTRAL HOTEL - owned/run by Lotzenhiser & Renbarger (7/25/89); is sold by A.B. Loutzenhiser to Cyrus Roose who comes to Fmt. from Cincinnati, OH (10/22/91)
CIGAR & TOBACCO SHOP - owned/operated by Daniel Moynihan (4/14/92)
CITIZEN'S EXCHANGE BANK - Nixon Winslow, Pres.; W.J. Leach, Vice Pres.; Will F. Brown, Cashier (3/20/96)
CITIZEN'S GAS CO. - Frank Davis is Supt., replacing Fred Macy who resigned (1/4/00)
CITIZEN'S TELEPHONE - S.B. Hill, mgr. (6/3/98); has 120 phone subscribers, can reach other towns by telephone; Miss Lesta Hasty, daytime operator; S.B. Hill and Walter Hardy take night calls (2/15/00); 130 telephones in operation (6/14/00); our phone lines now extend to Matthews (10/25/00)
COLUMBIA HOTEL - recently sold by J.W. Deaner to W. Welty (11/19/97); mgr., J.M. Lynch (12/29/98); new proprietor H.A. Scott is installing a bath tub in the hotel (2/16/99); was managed several yr ago by D.W.B. Marsh (dec) (3/23/99); - see Grand Hotel
CONNER DRUG STORE - started ca 1889 by W.B. Conner (4/14/92)
COOK'S GROCERY - Lonnie LaRue, employee (8/16/00)
COOPER LIVERY STABLE - on 9th St. across from Frazier Hotel; started ca 1888; owned/operated by Hiram Cooper (4/14/92)
CRYSTAL ICE PLANT - started making ice 10 Jul 1900 (7/12/00); mgr., H.E. Johnson (8/23/00); plant produces 75 tons of ice per wk, most is shipped elsewhere; Philip Hamm of Elwood is prop. (9/6/00)
CURRIE BROOD & SALE STABLE - owned by Gabriel Currie; has 5 draft horses at stud (4/14/92)
DALE HARDWARE - owned/operated by J.W. Dale; Alvin D. Bryan is the tinner (3/11/98); A.M. Pressnall is employee (3/18/98), and he now dies 30 Dec 1900 (12/31/00)
DICKINSON MEAT MARKET - bought by H.W. Dickinson from Newt Allen (4/19/00)
DAVISSON & SCOTT CLOTHING STORE - mentioned (4/14/92)
DILLON ADDITION - Allen Dillon is selling 138 bldg. lots (4/14/92)

FAIRMOUNT (continued)
DILLON GLASS WORKS - started production of glass 19 Apr 1891; Jack Cone is the blacksmith, Jake Bowers is a glassblower (4/23/91); George Coleman and Arthur Fleming, employees (7/2/91); 6 new tempering ovens are being constructed; large addition to packing room is built; new boiler and new engine to run grinding machine; new well is sunk (7/23/91); has 24 glass blowers, 12 on day shift, 12 on night shift (9/3/91); Henry Jones, employee (9/24/91); 10 young women are employed in grinding and finishing dept. (10/1/91); C.M. Tigner, employee (10/15/91); is shipping several RR cars of ware weekly (12/24/91); established by Allen Dillon; employs 125-150 men; J.H. Parker, Pres.; Levi Scott, Sec./Treas.; C.M. Tigner, General Manager (4/14/92)
DILLON'S RESTAURANT - owned/operated by Jesse Dillon (7/25/89)
EAGLE SHOE STORE - owned/operated by Jacob Beals (7/25/89; 4/14/92)
EASTES HARNESS SHOP - owned/operated by Charles Eastes (7/25/89); sells carriages, buggies and carts (8/8/89)
EDWARDS DRUG STORE - owned/operated by N.W. Edwards; H.L. Kepler is a jeweler in this store (7/25/89); established ca 1878; Orv W. Edwards, brother of owner, works here (4/14/92)
ENTERPRISE MANUFACTURING CO. - makes extension tables; employs 25 people (1/7/92)
FAIR STORE - owned/operated by E.P. Sissons (7/25/89)
FAIRMOUNT BRICK WORKS - Willis B.F. Moore (11/26/91), and C.D. Overman are owners/operators; employs 30 people; can make 25,000 bricks each day (4/14/92)
FAIRMOUNT CANNING CO. - Levi Scott is an owner; Jesse Scott, Supt. (3/24/92); last Monday received 1st load of tomatoes (8/25/92)
FAIRMOUNT CORONET BAND - gave an open-air concert on Christmas Day (12/31/91)
FAIRMOUNT FOUNDRY & MACHINE SHOP - owned/operated by brothers, W.F. and A.W. Fink (1/7/92; 4/14/92); A.W. Fink has sold out to W.F. Fink (4/21/92); manufactures 'Eureka' steel windmills (5/29/96)
FAIRMOUNT GLASS WORKS/RAU GLASS FACTORY - Fred and Charles Rau will work here; James Fischer is a 'gathering boy' (9/3/91); James Sharp is a glass blower (11/12/91); started in 1889; owned/operated by John Rau and W.C. Winslow (4/14/92); purchased last Saturday by John Rau for $17,035 (8/12/98); Lawrence McMaster is an employee (1/11/00)

FAIRMOUNT (continued)
FAIRMOUNT MEAT MARKET - owned/operated by H.W. Winslow and W.H. Hasting (4/14/92)
FAIRMOUNT MILLING CO./FAIRMOUNT MILLS - Frank Winks is head miller (2/7/89); Zep Gossett is engineer (10/22/91); Vint Cone is engineer while Zep Gossett is ill (10/29/91); firm is dissolved (5/5/92)
FAIRMOUNT MINING CO. - has 10 mi. of gas line serving natural gas to homes and business'; a malfunction caused the office bldg. of Wood & Sluder and the home of A. Hodson to burn down (1/14/92); is drilling a new gas well at 12th & N. Main Streets (12/6/00)
FAIRMOUNT POST OFFICE - Miss Myrtle Latham is Deputy Postmaster (7/25/89); f Postmaster Albert H. Johnson d 15 Dec 1891 in KY (1/7/92)
FAIRMOUNT RESTAURANT AND BAKERY - recently opened by M/M Richard McCandliss (7/7/92); C.M. Boyland, baker, is now a partner (8/11/92)
FAIRMOUNT WOOLEN MILL - does custom spinning and carding; in charge of W.S. Wardwell (4/18/89)
FARMER'S AND MERCHANT'S STATE BANK - Levi Scott, Cashier (7/25/89; 11/12/91); James Luther, Asst. Cashier (8/6/91; 11/5/91); L.R. Whitney, employee (10/8/91); stockholders were H.D. Reasoner, John D. Kirkwood, Ruth Elliott, Joseph W. Smiley, Thomas W. Newby, Ryland Ratliff, James Johnson, George W. Thurston, Thurza Howell; firm went bankrupt in 1893; Phillip Matter was appointed Trustee by the court and has now paid off the stockholders and creditors (1/11/00; 2/22/00)
FLANAGAN & DILLON'S STORE - sells millinery (10/27/92)
FLANAGAN & HENLEY'S STORE - employs Joshua Hollingsworth and Glen Henley (7/25/89)
FLINT & GOSSETT BLACKSMITH SHOP - new bldg.; owned by Elmer Flint and Will Gossett (5/1/96)
FORT BARBERSHOP - sold by Lige Fort recently to his brother, Sant Fort (3/5/91)
FRAZIER HOTEL - has 16 sleeping rooms, a parlor and a dining room; run by Mrs. S. Frazier since ca 1884 (4/14/92)
FRUIT MARKET - owned/operated by J. Marion Lemon (4/14/92)
GOSSETT & PHILLIPS MEAT MARKET - is now closed (6/22/99)
GRAND HOTEL - f called Columbia Hotel; prop. is H.A. Scott (10/19/99)
GROCERY STORE - owned by D.E. Allred (4/14/92)
GROCERY STORE - owned by Fred Oakley (4/14/92)

FAIRMOUNT (continued)
GUNSMITH SHOP - George Vaughn, gunsmith (4/23/91)
HAHN & O'MARA DRUG STORE - opened in the new Borrey Blk. last Wednesday (9/27/00)
HANE MEAT MARKET - owned by Adam Hane; is near Big Four Depot (11/3/98)
HARRIS CLOTHING STORE - owned by M. Harris (7/9/97)
HEADLEY GLASS FACTORY - is under construction (12/24/00)
HIATT FARM MACHINERY & VEHICLES STORE - owned/operated by M.A. Hiatt (7/25/89)
HIATT & FERREE HARNESS SHOP - sells hand-made harness (10/29/91)
HIPES' MEAT MARKET - owned/operated by John Hipes (7/25/89)
HOLLINGSWORTH MILLINERY SHOP - owned by Mrs. Mary Hollingsworth (3/27/96)
HUNT & FERREE FURNITURE STORE - recently established by John A. Hunt and John Ferree (4/10/96); John A. Hunt is a funeral director (6/18/97)
ICE & CO. DRY GOODS STORE - run by the brothers, Andy and Ben Ice (7/25/89)
JAQUES CLOTHING STORE - owned by F.M. Jaques (3/27/96)
JAY'S BARBER SHOP - recently purchased by Riley Jay from Lem Pemberton; barbers employeed by Jay are Loman McNeil and Bert Sherwin (7/2/97); business equipment is moved to Marion (4/15/98)
KEELY BOARDING HOUSE - run by Dolly Keely; the cook, Miss Pearl Roberts, was severely burned last Sunday (10/26/99)
KING CITY GLASS WORKS - Ed Tigner, mgr. (7/17/96)
KIRKPATRICK & CLARK MEAT MARKET - recently opened in bldg. one door W of Galloway's Restaurant (5/28/91); make good bologna (6/11/91); no longer in existence (4/14/92)
KLONDYKE MINING CO. - raising capital for Alaska gold mining at $25 per share (3/4/98)
LATHAM VEHICLE & HARNESS MANUFACTURING CO. - employs Gabe Johnson (7/25/89); owned by T.P. Latham; sells harness and buggies (4/14/92); has been purchased by Will E. Wilson (4/8/98)
LaRUE'S LIGHT PLANT - is furnishing electric power for lights in Congregational Ch. (3/4/98)
LINDSEY LUMBER MILL - owned/operated by W.H. Lindsey; employs 10 men (1/7/92; 4/14/92); sawmill burned, is being rebuilt (6/7/00); Henry Grindle is an employee (8/23/00)

FAIRMOUNT (continued)
LITTLE PLUMBING SHOP - owned/operated by Alex Little (4/14/92)
LONG HAND LAUNDRY - on W. Washington St.; operated by Sam Long, a Chinaman (9/22/98)
LONG'S STORE - owned/operated by A.R. Long (7/25/89)
LOWMAN & CONNER STORE - exists (7/25/89)
LUCAS RESTAURANT - baker is Fred Davis (3/30/99); clerk is Henry Charles (5/3/00); Clyde Gossett is an employee (9/6/00)
McCANDLESS Meat Market - recently purchased by J.E. Gates (4/17/96); owned/operated by McCandless & Gossett; Gossett sells his interest to McCandless recently (8/19/98)
McCULLOGH FACTORY - Martin Flanagan was night watchman until 28 Jul 1900 when he committed suicide (8/1/00)
McHENRY DRESSMAKING SHOP - owned/operated by Mrs. Maggie McHenry in residence of J.B. Smithson (4/14/92)
MILES PHOTOGRAPHY STUDIO - owned/operated by J.A. Miles (4/14/92; 5/22/96); Miss Leona Fink is an employee (5/22/96)
MILLER CANDY KITCHEN - recently opened by Charles Miller in N room of Sutton Blk. (1/4/00)
MILLER & HAAS DEPT. STORE - opened 1 wk ago (4/2/97); advertises in Fmt. News (7/2/97)
MILLINERY SHOP - owned by Mrs. M. Hollingsworth (4/14/92)
MILLINERY SHOP - owned by Mrs. N.A. Wilson; sells hats and bonnets (4/14/92)
MORRIS SALOON - blown up on night of 15 Aug 1893, then set afire the following night; Walter C. Rush, now in 1897 claims that he did it (9/3/97); saloon is closed (3/4/98); is opened as a licensed 'quart shop'(3/11/98); 'quart house' is closed (3/25/98)
NIXON GRAIN WAREHOUSE - owned/operated by T.J. Nixon (1/7/92)
NORTON GROCERY STORE - employs James Brown (7/25/89); owned by Major B.B. Norton (4/14/92)
OAKLEY'S EMPORIUM - employs Fred Oakley and Riley F. White (7/25/89)
ONE PRICE CLOTHING HOUSE - recently established by B. Kirschbaum (4/14/92)
OVERMAN BICYCLE REPAIR SHOP - on 1st St. is run by Edward Overman (5/3/00)
OVERMAN BRICK FACTORY - is being rebuilt (6/26/96) after being lost to fire last yr; owned by Clark D. Overman (10/15/97)
OVERMAN'S GENERAL MERCHANDISE STORE - owned/operated by C.D. Overman (7/25/89)

FAIRMOUNT (continued)
OVERMAN & MOORE - manufacture bricks (1/7/92)
PALACE MEAT MARKET - owned/operated by Haisley & Allen (4/14/92); N. Allen buys out the interest of his partner, Elwood Haisley (10/13/92)
PARKER'S OPERA HOUSE - is in Fmt. (1/29/97); has a magic show tonight, admission $0.20 for adults and $0.10 for children (2/5/97); Apr 16 will have 'Old Maid's Convention' (4/2/97); Town Board decides that license must be purchased for Opera House so owner J.H. Parker closed it to public meetings for which he has not been charging (8/27/97); may take out slanting floor and make Opera House into rental apartments; Parker investing $2,500 in rebuilding it some years ago but is not making much return on it (9/10/97); Wildwood Stock Co. to appear here next wk (9/17/97); matinee prices: $0.10 for children, $0.20 for adults (9/24/97); Fmt. IOOF Lodge sponsors 'Holiday Musicale' on 30 Dec 1897, admission $0.25 and $0.15 (12/24/97); since operation of the opera house has not been profitable recently, Asa Carter and son are hired to take up the slanting floor and re-lay it on the same level throughout (9/2/98); new floor is completed; a dance was held here Sat. night; Miss Amanda Weaver of Marion will give weekly dancing lessons here (9/29/98); Fmt. Catholic ladies will hold wk-long bazaar here starting 15 Feb 1899 (1/19/99); Sun. night one of the keystones over a front window fell to the pavement, two more were loose and were taken down (5/4/99); 18 Nov 1899 a dance is held in 'Parker's Hall' (11/23/99); 3 Feb 1900 K.O.T.M. will have a Grand Ball here (1/25/00)
PAYNE PLUMBING SHOP - owned/operated by Charles Payne (4/14/92)
L. PEARSON & CO. - employes 25 men; makes slack barrel staves (1/7/92; 4/14/92)
PEMBERTON FARM PRODUCE STORE - owned/operated by J.K. Pemberton (4/14/92)
PICKARD BROTHERS BLACKSMITH SHOP - burned 10 Mar 1891 (3/12/91); W.D. Pickard is an owner (4/14/92)
PICKARD MILLINARY SHOP - operated by Mary Pickard and her dt, Alice, in the north room of the Long Bldg. (4/16/91)
PIONEER DRUG STORE - owned by Nathan W. Edwards (1/31/96)
PLANING MILL & EXCELSIOR WORKS - owned by Gilbert LaRue & Co. employs 25 persons; ships 4 car-loads of product each wk (7/30/91; 4/14/92)

FAIRMOUNT (continued)
RABER FURNITURE STORE - owned/operated by Ed Raber (7/25/89); now is
RABER & ACKERMAN FURNITURE/UNDERTAKING PARLOR - E.J. Raber began ca 1887 (4/14/92); this business blk. burned 1 Oct 1892, with a loss of $20,000 to the various business' destroyed (10/6/92)
RAY & PEARSON REAL ESTATE - operated by A.W. Ray and W.R. Pearson (4/14/92)
RESTAURANT - owned/operated by A.W. Shuey and J.M. Bloomer who bought it from Galloway; also has boarders (4/14/92); Shuey sells out (10/13/92)
RICHARDS REAL ESTATE & INSURANCE - run by J.H. Richards who came to Fmt. ca 1888 (4/14/92)
ROBERTS HARNESS SHOP - owned/operated by J.W. Roberts (4/14/92)
RUDICIL'S SHAVING PARLOR - next door to Edward's Drug Store (4/16/97); was purchased by Joe Patenaude who will operate it (9/14/99)
SCOTT'S OPERA HOUSE - general admission tickets are $0.25; Congregational Ch. services are held here on Sundays (12/27/88); seats 600 people; owned by Levi Scott (4/14/92); heavily damaged by fire on 1 Oct 1892 (10/6/92)
SHOE SHOP - run by Micah Baldwin and Seth Cox (10/15/91)
SMALL'S HARDWARE/IMPLEMENT STORE - owned/operated by C.R. Small (7/25/89); now owned/operated by Elwood Davis and T.J. Lucas (4/14/92)
SMITHSON & BAKER CONTRACTING & BUILDING FIRM - owned/operated by J.B. Smithson and John S. Baker (4/14/92)
STARR FRUIT STAND - placed by C.A. Starr at Main & Washington St. (6/7/00); is moved from bank corner to Washington & Adams St. (6/14/00)
'THE OAK' BARBER SHOP - owned/operated by N.S. Fort and L.P. Pemberton (4/14/92)
SUTTON MILLINERY SHOP - to be opened 9 Apr 1900 by Mrs. Jennie Sutton in the Sutton Blk., S. Main St. (3/29/00)
WHEELER'S MILL - J.N. Wheeler also sells Pillsbury Flour (4/14/92)
WHITE HOUSE DEPT. STORE - H.C. Harris, prop.; will have grand opening 3 Oct 1891 (10/1/91)
WHITE HOUSE RESTAURANT - prop., W.A. Hurless (1/11/00); purchased by Esom O. Leach who will operate it (2/15/00)

FAIRMOUNT (continued)
WILEY & SWAIM LUMBER YARD - owned/operated by W.H. Wiley and J.L. Swaim (1/7/92; 4/14/92)
WILSON'S CORNER GROCERY - owned/operated by M/M Nate Wilson (7/25/89)
WILSON & MCCULLOGH GLASS FACTORY - Martin Flanagan was night watchman until 28 Jul 1900 when he committed suicide (8/1/00); makes fruit jars (10/4/00)
WINSLOW & RAU GLASS WORKS - see Fairmount Glass Works
WINSLOW & SONS LIVERY STABLES - owned/operated by H.W. Winslow and sons, John H. and Jabez N.; started ca 1874 (4/14/92); Sat. 1 Oct 1892 at 4:20 A.M., burned destroying 8 horses, several buggies and carriages, and Raber & Ackerman's hearse (10/6/92)
WOOD & SLUDER MILL - work on saw timber and ties (1/7/92); their office burned down due to a malfunction of the natural gas supply in their heating system (1/14/92); employes 30 to 50 men (4/14/92)
WORLEY GROCERY STORE - owned by J.W. Worley (4/14/92)
WRIGHT LAUNDRY - owned by Van Wright; has bath room; a free bath is given with each $0.25 of laundry (1/18/00)
ZINC SMELTING WORKS - was organized in Feb. 1899 (1/18/00); electric light plant installed here by electrician, William Bowers (4/20/99); Works were completely destroyed by fire 11 Jul 1899 (7/20/99); site was f a canning factory site (9/7/99)

FAIRMOUNT BASEBALL CLUB - 23 Sep 1897 defeated Marion Baseball Club (9/24/97)

FAIRMOUNT FAIR - will be held 16-20 Sept 1889 (7/25/89); fair grounds has a one-half mile track (9/5/89); will be held 10-14 Aug 1896 (7/3/96)

FAIRMOUNT FRIENDS ACADEMY (FFA) - Hannah Ellis to be in charge of new dormatory (9/3/91); Elwood O. Ellis is new Principal (9/17/91); tchr Will Calhoun resigns (3/31/92); vandals broke a door and drove in a cow the night of 1 Nov 1892 (11/3/92); bldg./ landscaping on Rush Street site cost $17,327.60 (3/27/96); E.O. Ellis, Supt./tchr (5/1/96); Vashti Binford, tchr (4/9/97); now has installed a telephone and can call downtown (10/15/97); Elam Henderson to replace Elwood O. Ellis as principal (6/3/98); Mrs. Conner of Phlox to have charge of the dormitory 1898-99

(8/26/98); Principal for 1900-01 is Prof. Wm. E. Schoonover of Brookville (8/23/00)

FAIRMOUNT GUN CLUB - recently formed with 12 mbrs including Earl Bryan, H.I. Wheeler, Lem Pemberton, John Bogue, Vall Roll, W.D. Bogue (6/26/96); Shoot participants each shoot 25 birds (7/3/96); 19 Oct 1897 held shoot at Fmt. Fair Grounds, winners were H.I. Wheeler, Elmer Hiatt, George Vaughn and Lem Pemberton (10/22/97); Club is re-activated by E.E. Hiatt and George W. Vaughn; 4 barrels of clay pigeons are purchased for shoots; other mbrs are P.C. Armstrong, W.A. Beasley, J.W. Davis, John Doyle, A.A. Driggs, Frank Downs, E.L. Kimes, John Maloy, R.H. Miller, Elwood Miller, John Montgomery, Luther Morris, H.M. Parker, C.T. Parker, J.H. Parker, J.A. Sullivan, W.E. Wilson; Elmer Hiatt won Shoot on 20 Sep 1899 (9/21/99); competing in the 3rd shoot of the season at Fair Grounds were Ed Kimes, Charles Parker, John Montgomery, George Fletcher, George Vaughn, Mark Parker, Elmer Hiatt, Harry Miller, Fred Seeley, Harry Wiley and M.D. Robinson (7/12/00); at shoot in Fair Grounds last Mon. PM winners were Mark Parker, Elmer E. Hiatt, Ed Kimes, George Vaughn and Charles Haugh (9/20/00); at shoot last Sat. winners were George Vaughn, John Montgomery, Elmer Hiatt, Mark Parker and John Davis (11/1/00)

FAIRMOUNT IOOF LODGE - mbr/officers include B.F. Parker, Walter Jay, E.L. Winslow, H. Rittenhouse, David D. Davis, M. Kimes, O. Crabb, A. Mendenhall, B. Smith, S. Smithson, H. Haisley, A.M. Presnall, D. Haisley, Gabriel Johnson (1/4/00)

FAIRMOUNT PUBLIC LIBRARY - Isaiah Jay recently donated the 'Universal History,' a 21 volume set published 150 yr ago; 2 of the volumes are damaged by worms (5/12/97)

FAIRMOUNT PUBLIC SCHOOLS - Homer Dickey will teach this fall (9/3/91); 1st grade tchr is Mrs. Ella B. Carroll (11/12/91); Fmt. HS includes 6 rooms and Principal's Office built in 1891 at cost of $15,000; Principal is Elwood O. Ellis [?] (4/14/92); tchrs include Miss Geneva Sanders and Miss Lucy Parrill (4/2/97); Robert W. Himelick is Supt. (4/9/97); Sch Board mbrs are N.W. Edwards, F.H. Macy, Gabriel Johnson (6/15/99); 1899-1900 Elementary Sch tchrs are Mattie Charles, Anna Freeman, Minta Life, Maggie Lindley, Dea Nolder, Lucie Parrill (8/24/99); Michael Edward Monahan, Fmt. HS Principal for last 3 yr d recently

(1/26/99; 2/2/99); Grammar Sch tchrs are Dorothy Luther, Alice Nixon, Geneva Sanders, Osha Starr (8/24/99); 1899-1900 HS tchrs are Lillian P. Bassett, Xen Edwards, Maggie Baker, M.N. Hadley, W.L. Jay (8/24/99); 1900 HS grads are Grace B. Hobbs, Albert D. Knight, Inez Marven Hardwick, Grace Maxine Crilley, Irvin B. Winslow, John Porter Starr, Sarah Eliza Frazier and William Moses Morrison (5/10/00); new brick bldg. costing $8,000 will be placed at South Bldg. where dormitory stood (8/23/00)

FAIRMOUNT REBECCA LODGE 305 - Mrs. Martha Bowers is a mbr (1/11/00)

FAIRMOUNT TOWNSHIP - Kelsay Brothers found limestone 2 mi. S of Fmt. at depth of 4 feet; to mine this stone for constuction and road building they leased 120 acres over the stone on farms owned by Eli Neal, Robert Trader and Ed Woolen (12/17/91); only toll road left in Grant Co. Is 2.5 mi. segment of Fmt.-Summitville Pike from Fmt. S to the county line; Co. Commissioners may buy this last toll road; road from Fmt. to Jonesboro is no longer a toll road (12/15/98); Trustee Joseph Ratliff will have a new Fowlerton Sch built (4/20/99)

FAIRMOUNT TOWNSHIP SCHOOLS - 1891-92 term starts (9/3/91); 1st Twp. Commencement was held in Fmt. in 1883 by Elwood O. Ellis (6/28/00); Commencement to be held at Bethel M.P. Ch. on June 11th at 2:00 PM, Rev. Iliff to give invocation, Gervais Carey, speaker (6/10/98); graduation to be held in Pleasant Grove M.P. Ch. 9 Jun 1899 with four grads: Bert Carroll, Blanche Duling, Willie Jones, Edna Overman (6/1/99); Commencement to be 2 Jun 1900 in Hopewell Ch. at Leach (5/24/00)
DISTRICT # 1 (BACK CREEK) - Will Calhoun to be tchr this fall (4/18/89); large number of students att (11/7/89); 52 pupils are enrolled, 46 att (12/5/89); Homer Dickey, tchr (4/2/91); Roland T. Whitney, tchr (9/10/91); R.T. Whitney quit as tchr, O. Frank Dickey is now the tchr (10/8/91; 12/17/91); a spelling match was held here last Monday night (10/29/91); Verling Davis, tchr (8/31/99)
DISTRICT # 2 (PIKE) - 55 pupils enrolled; C.T. Parker, tchr (12/5/89);1898-99 tchr, Miss Gertrude Henshaw of Amboy (4/13/99)
DISTRICT # 3 (GRANT) - 52 students; Roland T. Whitney, tchr (12/5/89); Charles M. Hobbs, tchr (9/3/91)

FAIRMOUNT TOWNSHIP SCHOOLS (continued)
DISTRICT # 4 (EAST BRANCH) - J.W. Jones, tchr; has 69 pupils on some days (11/21/89); 70 pupils on roll (12/5/89); tchr Frank Sherwin (1/1/91), who now resigns and is replaced by J. Livesy (1/8/91; 3/19/91); Frank Sherwin, tchr (9/3/91); to join Lake Sch in Bethel M.P. MH for literary exercises on Thanksgiving Day (11/17/92); Murt Woollen, tchr (9/21/99); Miss __ Macon (dec) was a student (11/16/99); Murt Woollen, 1900-01 tchr, has 30 pupils (9/13/00)
DISTRICT # 5 (LEACHBURG) - 1900-01 tchr John Little is starting his 7th yr here (8/30/00)
DISTRICT # 6 (LAKE) - 34 students enrolled; Milo Ratliff, tchr (12/5/89); Calvin C. Rush, 1898-99 tchr (2/2/99)
DISTRICT # 7 (LIBERTY) - 34 pupils enrolled; Charles Hobbs, tchr (12/5/89), and is still tchr (3/19/91); 1898-99 tchr, Oscar B. Hockett (3/30/99); a new sch to be built in Fowlerton (4/20/99); a good water well was drilled here on 3rd try (1/18/00)
DISTRICT # 8 (LEACHBURG) - 41 pupils enrolled; J.H. Dean, tchr (12/5/89); William Ware, tchr (3/19/91; 9/3/91)

FANKBONER, Osmond - s Lewis Fankboner, farmer near Fmt. (2/12/91)

FAVORS, Mack - left for KS this wk to help thresh wheat (6/28/00)

FEAR, James 'Ned' - age 55; of 0.75 mi. W of Fmt.; injured when his team ran away, d 17 May 1899 (5/18/99)

FEAR, Mrs. Z.W. - of Summitville; dt Rachel C. (Vestal) Petty of Fmt. (1/21/98)

FELLOW, Anna (Baldwin) - of Tipton Co.; dt Thomas and Lydia Baldwin (5/25/99)

FELLOWS, __ - see Mrs. Frank B. ZEIGLER

FELLOWS, Willard Emory - b Essex Co., NY 20 Oct 1815; m Sophronia Kirkland 19 Mar 1844; father of Mrs. F.B. Zeigler; d 19 Dec 1898 (12/22/98)

FELTON, Oscar - age 28; s Benjamin Felton of Upland; m; 25 Feb 1899 caved in the skull of Ed Chance while both were working at Zinc Smelting Works, Upland; he was arrested (3/2/99)

FERGUSON, Jesse - of Upland area; recently assaulted his landlord, Jesse Johnson (1/29/97)

FERREE, Evan H. - of Marion is s M/M John Ferree (2/12/97)

FERREE, John - att Earlham Coll (9/10/91); named as 1896-97 Fmt. HS tchr (3/6/96); establishes Hunt & Ferree Furniture Store with partner John A. Hunt (4/10/96)

FERREE, William - att Purdue Univ (1/1/91; 3/19/91)

FIELDS, Rev. W.S. - lives in Gas City (9/27/00)

FINK, __ - see Mrs. Wilson BOGUE

FINK, J.R. - Hackleman storekeeper was given party for his 43rd birthday 13 Jul 1898 by his wife and dt (7/15/98)

FINK, Miss Leona - employed in Miles Photography Studio (5/22/96)

FINK, W.F. - and brother, A.W. Fink owns/operates Fmt. Foundry & Machine Shops (4/14/92); bought out A.W. Fink (4/21/92)

FINNEY, Frances - see Jacob Reese WRIGHT

FISCHER, James - employed as a 'gathering boy' by Winslow & Rau Glass Works (9/3/91)

FISHER, Jake - 19 Jan 1896 m Minnie Morris, both of Fmt. (1/17/96)

FLANAGAN, Martin - landholder advertising 'no hunting' on his property (10/13/92); m; night watchman at McCullogh Factory; d 28 Jul 1900 after cutting his own throat with his pocket knife; bur Park Cem (8/1/00)

FLEMING, Arthur - an employee of Dillon Glass Works (7/2/91); granted license to sell liquor in Fmt.; is 4th liquor retailer now in town (9/22/98)

FLETCHER, George A. - Fmt. Town Clerk (1/18/00); a winner in 3rd shoot of season at Fmt. Gun Club (7/12/00)

FLINN, John - age 17; d last wk (8/23/00)

FLINT, Elmer - purchases blacksmith shop from Frank Swope; Frank Lottridge is his employee (12/27/88); moves into new blacksmith shop with his partner Will Gossett (5/1/96); has dissolved his partnership with Will Gossett (3/12/97)

FLOYD, Mr. __ - from Clinton Co. will teach in Pansy Sch (10/13/92)

FORT, __ - baby of M/M Sant Fort; d 11 May 1889, bur BC Friends Cem (5/16/89)

FORT, Charles - returns to his Jonesboro home after spending 6 yr in Indiana State Prison (3/11/98)

FORT, Lige - recently sold his barbershop to his brother, Sant; moves to Muncie (3/5/91)

FORT, N.S. - and L.P. Pemberton owns 'The Oak' Barber Shop (4/14/92)

FORT, Sant - Fmt. barber; recently bought barbershop from his brother (3/5/91)

FOUSE, Mrs. James - see Rachel (Modlin) LITTLE

FOUSE, Maggie - see J.C. LONG

FOUST, Ralph - working on farm 7.5 mi. W of Fmt.; killed in a hunting accident 24 Jun 1896 (6/26/96)

FOWLER, __ - see Mrs. Charles W. SMITH

FOWLER, Jessie (Norton) - of Jonesboro; dt Major B.V. Norton; m Jot Fowler (1/7/98)

FOWLER, Louis - age 16; of Gas City; 6' 3" tall; d last Sun from a swimming accident in Mississinewa River (8/6/97)

FOWLERTON (f called LEACH) - Fowler Brothers manufacture clay drainage tile (3/13/96); town to have glass factory employing 150 men by 1 Sep 1896, to be built by Fowlerton citizens on 15 acres donated by William J. Leach, Fowler boys will donate gas from their well (4/17/96); Frank Norton starts a store with James Brown as head clerk (7/31/96); Sol Key is a barber; Ed Smith is a shoemaker/cobbler; Roll Council has a blacksmith shop (3/12/97; 4/16/97); is on C.I.&E. RR (8/1/00)

FRAZIER, __ - dwarf dt William Frazier; d 5 Oct 1892 (10/6/92)

FRAZIER, Allie - 5 Apr 1889 was given party for his 15th birthday (4/11/89)

FRAZIER, Ananias - 27 Mar 1889 filed for divorce from wife, Cora J.; they have a 5 yr old son (3/28/89); last Sat. m a white woman in Hartford City (3/24/92); is an evangelist; white wife was Miss __ Runk (5/12/92); is a Fmt. barber (4/30/97)

FRAZIER, Benjamin - mbr Fmt. Friends boy's SS class (1/11/00); s Mrs. Sallie Frazier; att 2-yr law course at Marion Normal Coll (9/6/00)

FRAZIER, Clarkson Leslie - of S of Fmt.; b 16 Aug 1874; s Elihu and Rachel; m; d 20 Jun 1896, bur Park Cem (6/26/96)

FRAZIER, Mrs. S. - started operating Frazier Hotel ca 1884 (4/14/92)

FRAZIER, Sarah Eliza - colored; grad Fmt. HS 1900 (5/10/00)

FRAZIER, William A. - b Culpepper Co., WV 25 Dec 1828; m 2 Oct 1857 Mary Burden, dt Austin and Emily Burden; d 7 Jan 1901 (1/7/01)

FREEMAN, Anna - Fmt. Schs 1896-97 3rd grade tchr (3/6/96); 1899-1900 Fmt. Elementary Sch tchr (8/24/99)

FREEMAN, Elizabeth - see Lindsey BULLER

FREER, Mrs. Lottie - see Edmund SEALE

FRIEND, Eliza - mbr Fmt. Women's Relief Corps (11/14/89)

FRIEND, Ida - see Iredel MARLEY

FRIEND, M.S. - of Fmt.; CW vet (3/29/89), serv Co. C, 12th Ind. Inf. (9/5/89); Deputy Prosecutor for Fmt. Twp. (7/2/91); officer, Beeson Post, GAR (12/10/91)

FRIES, Charlotte - see Charlotte PEACOCK

FRITCH, Samuel - and W.E. Gossett own a Fmt. blacksmith shop (4/14/92)

FULTZ, Mrs. William - d 22 Jan 1889 (1/24/89)

GALATIA CREEK DITCH, KELSAY BRANCH - near Lake Galatia in Fmt. Twp.; Albert Compton contracted to dig this ditch for $925 (2/1/00)

GALLIMORE, Daniel W. - purchases Riley Jay Barber Shop (11/12/91); has a Barber Shop & Bath Room (4/14/92)

GAMBRIEL, J.R. - of Liberty Twp.; serv 34th Ind. Inf. 28 Aug 1861 to 3 Feb 1866 (9/24/91)

GARDNER, Elizabeth - see Elizabeth BROYLES

GARDNER, Henry - lives in Fmt.; serv Co. K, 130th Regmt. Ind. Vol. Inf. during CW (9/15/92); att his Unit Reunion in Elwood 6 Aug 1896 (8/7/96)

GARNER, Elwood - 20 Jun 1891 m Louie Rush (6/25/91)

GARNER, Leota - 1891 grad of a Liberty Twp. sch (5/21/91)

GARNER, Ruth (Haisley) - dt Ira and Rebecca Haisley (9/10/97)

GAS CITY - Frank Leslie's Illustrated Newspaper will soon publish write-up of this town (12/27/88); J.M. Lynch has leased the Mississinewa Hotel (1/12/99)

GAS WELLS - there are 6 in Fmt. (2/5/97); a gas well is being drilled on farm of John Seale (8/1/00); Ind. Natural Gas & Oil Co. just completed a fine gas well on the farm of John Caskey (9/20/00)
BACK CREEK GAS WELL - located N of BC Friends MH; new wellhouse and regulator house were built, gas is piped S to South Toll Gate (11/19/91); a connection burst on Mon. allowing the escape of much gas; Alex Little repaired it (2/11/92)
H.A. JONES FARM GAS WELL - the Gas City Co. is drilling a gas well on the H.[Hiram] A. Jones farm by the Lake Sch House (10/13/92)

GASKEY, Mrs. Etta - has gone to St. Louis where she will attend medical coll (9/15/92)

GATES, J.E. - purchases the McCandless Meat Market (4/17/96)

GATES, Mary Louisa (Wescott) - b Dearborn Co. 5 Mar 1865; m Elmore Gates 24 Jun 1886; mbr Methodists; d 5 Jun 1897 (6/18/97)

GAUNTT, Reuel Julian - long-time resident of Liberty Twp.; b Green Co., TN 17 Jul 1824; s Samuel K. and Precious Gauntt; m Grant Co. 7 Nov 1847 Sarah Beals (b Green Co., TN; d 8 Apr 1879); father of Marion Postmaster; d 27 Jul 1889, bur West Ridge Cem, Liberty Twp. (8/1/89)

GIBSON, infant - child of George Gibson, glassblower; d 19 Aug 1897 (8/20/97)

GIBSON, __ - child of M/M Bert Gibson; d last Monday (11/22/00)

GIBSON, Mrs. Dan - of Jonesboro; d recently (3/25/98)

GIBSON, Flossie - dt George Gibson (5/28/91)

GIBSON, George W. - of Jonesboro; is awarded a CW military pension (2/5/91)

GIBSON, Helen D. (Rush) - is suing Milton A. Gibson for divorce (5/18/99)

GIBSON, John - lives at Jonesboro; serv Co. K, 130th Regmt. Ind. Vol. Inf. during CW (9/15/92); CW vet bur in BC Friends Cem (6/5/96)

GIBSON, Milton A. - student that Frank McCoy was found guilty of mistreating (4/21/92); of Weaver area; 25 Dec 1898 m Helen D. Rush, dt M/M J.F. Rush of Fmt. (12/29/98); is sued for divorce by Helen (5/18/99)

GIBSON, Mrs. Oren - of Matthews; dt William Elliott of Hackleman (5/10/00)

GIFT, C.W. - landholder advertising 'no hunting' on his property (10/13/92)

GIFT, Zenethen Kelsey - b 3 Oct 1899; s Henry E. and Estella E.; d 17 Aug 1900 (8/23/00)

GILLISPIE, Hen - recently killed a black rattlesnake near Lake Galatia (7/2/91)

GLASS, D.D. - left for KS this wk to help thresh wheat (6/28/00)

GLASS, Mrs. David - of E of Fmt.; d 18 Dec 1899, bur Park Cem (12/21/99)

GLESSNER, Al - s John Glessner of Maple Run Friends area; without provocation, was shot and wounded in the forehead by the drunken 23-yr-old Albert Silvers on 21 Apr 1900 in Coles [Station]; a warrant has been issued for Silvers arrest (4/26/00)

GLOVER, Will - blacksmith in Big Four Window Glass Factory (8/23/00)

GOBLE, Will - tchr, Green Twp. Dist. # 8 Sch (12/5/89); and wife are new mbrs of Center Christian Ch. (3/31/92)

GOODYKOONTZ, Jonathan - of Jonesboro; age ca 36; s Abraham (dec); d 14 Jul 1896 (7/31/96)

GORDON, Rev. D.F. - pastor, Fmt. W.M. Ch. (6/8/99)

GORTON, Elsie - b ca 3 Apr 1886; dt M/M W.E. Gorton; d 17 Aug 1889 (8/22/89)

GOSSETT, Clyde - works in Lucas Restaurant (9/6/00)

GOSSETT, El. - and others are laying foundation of new Fmt. Baptist MH (12/17/91); contracted to do stone work on new Little Ridge Sch (3/24/92)

GOSSETT, [Ella] Emma - see William E. GOSSETT

GOSSETT, Henry M. - of Decatur, IL; s Milton and Ruth (Killen) Gossett (7/18/89)

GOSSETT, Isaac N. - is in meat business in Indianapolis with Richard McCandless (5/8/96); sold his interest in Fmt. meat market to McCandless since Gossett recently sawed off a thumb while cutting meat (8/19/98); and family moved to Gas City (7/27/99)

GOSSETT, Jessie - dt M/M Z.M. Gossett; had 7th birthday party 14 Jul 1900 (7/19/00)

GOSSETT, John L. - of Sardinia, OH; s Milton and Ruth (Killen) Gossett (7/18/89)

GOSSETT, Minnie - files for divorce from Will Gossett (1/29/91)

GOSSETT, Milton - b 2 May 1808 Highland Co., OH; s John and Ellen Gossett; m 1st Ruth Killen (dec) on 4 June 1830; m 2nd 14 July 1843 Naomi Pettijohn of Brown Co., OH; mbr Friends since 1883; d last wk, bur BC Friends Cem (7/18/89)

GOSSETT, Naomi (Pettijohn) - m Milton Gossett 14 July 1843 (7/18/89); 26 Jan 1891 was given party for 76th birthday (1/29/91)

GOSSETT, William E. - and Samuel Fritch own a Fmt. blacksmith shop (4/14/92); is employed in a Hackleman blacksmith shop; 18 Oct 1889 m [Ella] Nose of Jonesboro (10/24/89); now is a blacksmith in Independence (10/31/89); m [Ella] Emma Gossett 18 Jul

1891, both of Fmt. (7/23/91); moves into his new blacksmith shop with partner Elmer Flint (5/1/96); is no longer in partnership with E. Flint (3/12/97)

GOSSETT, Mrs. Z.M. - dt Jesse E. And Hannah (Hill) Wilson (4/13/99)

GOSSETT, Zep - is engineer for Fmt. Mills (10/22/91)

GRAND ARMY of the REPUBLIC (G.A.R.)- Beeson Post No. 386 in Fmt. - Post officers are Enoch Beals, Thomas Jones, John F. Jones, J.W. Curtis, J.B. Smithson, W.H. Smith, F.M. Wood, Gabriel Johnson, M.S. Friend and Alex Deering (12/10/91)

GRANT COUNTY, Schools - 1st Co. Commencement was held in Marion First Friends MH in 1888 by Elwood O. Ellis, Co. Supt. of Schools (6/28/00)

GRAY, __ - b 6 Oct 1889; s M/M Ben Gray (10/10/89)

GRAY, B.B. - mbr Fmt. W.M SS (9/26/89)

GRAY, Jermina Jane (Carter) - b Lee Co., IA 8 Jan 1863; dt Asa and Agnes Carter; m Benjamin Gray; mbr W.M. Ch.; d Fmt. 23 Dec 1890, bur Park Cem (12/25/90; 1/1/91)

GRAY, Lillian - b Preble Co., OH 20 July 1887; dt M/M Frank Gray; d 22 Oct 1889, bur Park Cem (10/24/89)

GREEN, William - age 111; d 10 Nov 1898 in Jonesboro home of his son-in-law Chris Swafford (11/17/98)

GREEN TOWNSHIP, Schools - 1896 graduation is held in Pt. Isabel for grads Earl Pyle, Roscoe Armstrong, Alonzo Shull, Ethel Matchette and Hattie Brand (6/5/96)
DISTRICT # 7 (PT. ISABEL) - tchr is James F. Hood (12/5/89)
DISTRICT # 8 - tchr is Will Goble (12/5/89)

GREENMAN, Rev. A. - pastor, Fmt. M.E. Ch. (5/19/92); due to ill health, resigns pastorate (8/25/92)

GREGG, David - 13 June 1889 m Nora Cox (6/20/89)

GREGG, Fay - infant dt David and Nora (Cox) Gregg; d recently (10/1/91)

GREY, Mrs. Oskie - dt Lydia J. (Leavelle) Taylor (6/7/00)

GRINDLE, Francis 'Frank' A. - b 16 Aug 1877; s M/M Benjamin A. Grindle; mbr West Milton, OH Friends; d 20 Feb 1897 (2/26/97)

GRINDLE, Henry - employee, Lindsay's sawmill (8/23/00)

HACKETT, Bessie Beatrice (Brown) - m William F. Hackett 29 Aug 1899; will live in Rochelle, IL where husband is a jeweler (8/31/99)

HACKLEMAN - J.R. Fink is a storekeeper (7/15/98); Frank McCabe is new postmaster (1/26/99)

HADLEY, M.N. - 1899-1900 Fmt. HS tchr (8/24/99)

HAILEY, Chris - employed by Hiatt Farm Machinery & Vehicle Store (7/25/89)

HAINES[HAYNES], F.M. - mbr, Bethel M.P. Ch. (4/16/97)

HAINES, M.M. - mbr, Union U.B. Ch. (4/16/97)

HAINES, Mrs. Norton - of Upland d last wk (1/10/89)

HAISLEY, Clinton - 18 Apr 1891 m Cora Cox (4/23/91)

HAISLEY, Mrs. Clint - of W of Jonesboro; 27 May 1900 is given party for her 28th birthday (5/31/00)

HAISLEY, D. - mbr/officer Fmt. IOOF (1/4/00)

HAISLEY, Dennis - appointed Liberty Twp. Trustee last wk to replace Dr. I.N. Seale (9/22/98)

HAISLEY, Ella - see Oliver HOCKETT

HAISLEY, Ellen - see Ellen CAREY

HAISLEY, Elva - Deer Creek Sch, Mill Twp. tchr (3/19/91); of Oak Ridge (10/15/91); - see J.B. SEALE

HAISLEY, Elwood - sells his interest in the Palace Meat Market to his partner, N. Allen (10/13/92); b Wayne Co. 1838; s Ira and Rebecca; came to Grant Co. 1839; m Millicent Rush 24 Aug 1858; d 2 Sep 1897, bur Park Cem (9/3/97; 9/10/97)

HAISLEY, H. - mbr/officer Fmt. IOOF (1/4/00)

HAISLEY, Jesse - s Ira and Rebecca (9/10/97)

HAISLEY, Linais - mbr BC Friends (4/16/97)

HAISLEY, Mary - see Mary MILLER

HAISLEY, Millicent (Rush) - V. Pres., Fmt. WCTU (9/15/98); 11 Oct 1899 given party for her 61st birthday (10/12/99)

HAISLEY, Minnie - of near Bethel is given party for her 17th birthday 1 Dec 1900 (12/6/00)

HAISLEY, Otto - mbr Fmt. Friends boy's SS class (1/11/00)

HAISLEY, Rebecca (Overman) - b Preble Co., OH 10 May 1819; dt Jessie and Keziah Overman; 23 Mar 1837 m Ira Haisley; came to Grant Co. in 1838; mbr Oak Ridge Friends; d 19 Feb 1897 (2/26/97)

HAISLEY, Ruth - see Ruth GARNER

HAISLEY, Sylvester - Oak Ridge Sch tchr (12/5/89); s Elwood Haisley (dec) (9/3/97)

HAISLEY, Waldo - grad-Ind. Law Sch; admitted to the bar (6/3/98); shares a Fmt. law office with Sylvester Haisley (6/10/98)

HAISLEY, Walter - att Indianapolis Dental Coll (10/15/97)

HAISLEY, Wash. - awarded a CW pension of $8 per month (4/23/91)

HALEY, Washington - CW vet bur in Park Cem (6/5/96)

HALL, David - of Marion; s William Hall (10/11/00)

HALL, Lee - of Marion; s Rev. William Hall (9/10/91; 10/11/00)

HALL, Mrs. Marion - dt M/M John Hipes, d 18 Jun 1891 (6/25/91)

HALL, Mary - see Mary HOLLINGSWORTH

HALL, Retta - mbr Fmt. Baptist Ch. (4/16/97)

HALL, Rev. William - of Fmt.; given party 28 Feb 1889 for his 76th birthday (3/7/89); grandson of John Gillaspie of NC (5/16/89); brother of Levi Hall of Xenia (7/18/89); came to Fmt. ca 1837; serv Ind. Legislature in 1861; d 4 Oct 1900, bur Park Cem (10/11/00)

HAMM, Philip - lives in Elwood; prop., Crystal Ice Plant (9/6/00)

HAMMOND, Frank - Asst. Supt., Fmt. Friends SS (7/9/91); b Henry Co. 8 Nov 1870; s Thomas and Catharine Hammond; came to Grant Co. ca 1885; mbr Friends; d 2 Sep 1899, bur Park Cem (9/7/99)

HAMMOND, [Katharine B.] 'Kate' - mbr Fmt. Friends Women's Foreign Missionary Society (11/26/91); 13 Oct 1898 was given surprise party for her 60th birthday (10/20/98)

HANCOCK, Cal. - landowner near Fmt. advertising that he permits no hunting on his property (11/12/97)

HANE, Adam, Sr. - m; has meat market near Big Four Depot (11/3/98)

HANE, Adam L., Jr. - b Red Key 29 Sep 1894; s M/M Adam Hane, Sr.; d 1 Nov 1898 (11/3/98; 11/10/98)

HARDWICK, Inez Marven - grad Fmt. HS 1900 (5/10/00)

HARDWICK, Miss Vernie - att DePauw Univ (5/24/00)

HARDY, Hiram - mbr Fmt. Friends boy's SS class (1/11/00)

HARDY, Walter - employee of Citizens Telephone Co.; is night and weekend operator along with S.B. Hill, mgr. (2/15/00)

HARRIS, Burr M. - appointed Postmaster of newly established Gas City Post Office (4/28/92)

HARRIS, H.C. - prop., White House Dept. Store (10/1/91; 4/14/92)

HARRIS, M. - owns a clothing store (7/9/97)

HARRISON, Luther - 8 Jan 1896 m Mrs. George Leach (1/17/96)

HARROLD, William - 13 Mar 1899 m Rhoda Martin; lives in Hackleman area (3/16/99)

HART, Jesse - left for KS this wk to help thresh wheat (6/28/00)

HARTLY, Sarah -see Mrs. Sarah SEELY

HARVEY, Austin - will deliver mail on Fmt. Rural Route No. 1 (3/29/00)

HARVEY, Eli - d 6 May 1891, bur Little Ridge Cem (5/7/91)

HARVEY, Enos - pastor, Fmt. Friends (1/29/97)

HARVEY, Ethel - 10 Oct 1898 was given party for her 18th birthday (10/13/98)

HARVEY, Ida - see Charles KNIGHT

HARVEY, Jane (Kelly) - b Waynesville, OH 17 Feb 1826; dt Timothy and Avis Kelly; 1845 m Henry Harvey (dec ca 1894) in BC Friends MH; d 4 Nov 1900 Williston, FL, bur beside husband in Orange Hill Cem, FL (11/15/00; 11/22/00)

HARVEY, John - mbr Fmt. Friends boy's SS class (1/11/00)

HARVEY, John W. - of 3 mi. W of Fmt. in Liberty Twp.; recently injured in corn shredder accident (11/30/99)

HARVEY, Mrs. Mahlon - d 24 Sept 1889 (9/26/89)

HARVEY, Thomas - prominent early settler in Fmt. Twp. (1/7/92)

HASTING, __ - see Mrs. Will DANIELS; also - see Mrs. Fremont ROUSH

HASTING, Alta Smith - b Grant Co. 13 Dec 1872; s Robert and Annie Hasting; d 24 Mar 1899, bur Park Cem (3/30/99)

HASTING(S), Mrs. Carter - age ca 76; mbr United Brethren Ch.; d 28 Jul 1889, bur BC Friends Cem (8/1/89)

HASTING, Daisy - dt M/M Robert Hasting (3/6/96)

HASTING, Mossie - see John B. DAVIS

HASTING, W.H. - with H.W. Winslow, owns Fmt. Meat Market (4/14/92)

HASTING, William - b Grant Co. 57 yr ago; d 30 May 1896, bur Park Cem (6/5/96)

HASTING, Wit - s M/M Robert Hasting (7/10/96)

HASTY, Miss Lesta - is daytime operator at Fmt. Telephone Exchange (6/8/99); resigned from telephone company (4/12/00)

HASTY, Robert - of Fmt. area; age 56; d 8 Mar 1889 (3/14/89)

HAUGH, Charles - a winner in Fmt. Gun Club shoot last Monday (9/20/00)

HAWORTH, Nora (Coppock) - lives in Fmt.; dt of Calvin Coppock (9/15/98)

HAYNES, __ - dt b to M/M Adam Haynes recently (6/8/99)

HAYNES, Madison Matthew - farmer of 2.5 mi. S of Fmt.; b Franklin Co. 22 Oct 1844; youngest s Solomon and Chloe Haynes; ca 1862 m Rebecca A. Lewis (dec 19 May 1878); m 2nd Sarah Pyle 10 Oct 1883; mbr United Brethren Ch.; d 18 Nov 1900, bur BC Friends Cem (11/22/00)

HAYWORTH, __ - contractor for construction of Clodfelter Electric Line (6/26/96)

HAYWORTH/HAWORTH, Hollis - mbr 160th Ind. Regmt. (11/10/98); is in camp in Columbus, GA (1/12/99)

HEAL, Elmer E. - moves this wk from Fmt. to Wheeling, Delaware Co.; will teach sch in Jefferson Twp. (6/27/89)

HEAL, William E. - Marion mathematician; is published in 'Annals of Mathematics,' monthly publication of American Association for Advancement of Science (12/10/91); candidate for Grant Co. Treas. (1/7/92); Grant Co. Treasurer, is short in his accounts but losses are covered by his personal note (1/3/96); resigns 23 Jan 1896 as Co. Treasurer (1/24/96); returned to Marion from Pittsburgh, PA to face charges of mishandling County funds (11/16/99)

HECK, Mrs. Ida - of Rigdon; is dt Mrs. Henry Pearson (4/13/99)

HEFREN, John - Jonesboro tailor; shot and wounded Lafe Johnson while both were drunk (7/25/89)

HENDERSON, Elam - Principal, Central Sch, Lawrence, KS; replaces Elwood O. Ellis as FFA Principal (6/3/98)

HENLEY, Alexander - b Randolph Co., NC 26 Jan 1832; s John and Margaret; conscripted into Confederate Army, allowed to work in State Salt Works near Wilmington, NC; he escaped and came to Fmt.; mbr Fmt. Friends; d 7 Apr 1900 (4/12/00)

HENLEY, Dr. Alpheus - brother of John Henley of KS (9/19/89); mbr, Fmt. Congregational Ch. bldg. committee (12/19/89); mbr, Fmt. Friends bldg. committee (2/11/92); his house is charred and his stable is burned in the fire of 1 Oct 1892 that also burned several Fmt. business' (10/6/92)

HENLEY, Elizabeth W. - see Elizabeth W. SEALE,

HENLEY, Dr. Glenn - employed by Flanagan & Henley's Store (7/25/89); 1896-97 att Univ of Michigan (7/2/97); Univ of Michigan medical student (10/1/97; 9/29/98); now has an X-ray apparatus in the medical office he shares with Dr. Alpheus Henley (7/12/00)

HENLEY, Jane - see Jane WINSLOW

HENLEY, Keziah - see Keziah DILLON

HENLEY, Louisa - mbr Fmt. WCTU (8/8/89)

HENLEY, Mary E. - see Mrs. Mary E. WOOD

HENLEY, Penina - see Jesse WINSLOW

HENLEY, Phineus - b 1802 in NC; m Mary Bogue (b 1802 in NC) (12/5/89)

HENLEY, Richard - employed in Fmt. News office (8/15/89)

HENLEY, Sarah (Newby) - b Grant Co. 25 Apr 1834; m John R. Henley 3 Mar 1851; mbr Spring Grove Friends, Miami Co., KS; d 4 Nov 1900 near Lebo, KS, bur Lincoln Cem, KS (11/15/00)

HENLEY, Will - s Milton Henley, f of Fmt.; is a mine overseer in N. China (11/1/00)

HENRY, Charles L. - mgr., Union Traction Co. (8/23/00)

HENSHAW, __ - see Mrs. John H. BUMPAS

HENSHAW, George J. - b Rush Co. 7 Jul 1833; m Sarah E. Oldacre 13 Feb 1857; mbr GAR; d Liberty Twp. 30 Dec 1898, bur Park Cem (1/5/99)

HENSHAW, Miss Gertrude - of Amboy was 1898-99 Pike Sch tchr (4/13/99)

HENSHAW, H.P. - stockholder in Winslow Glass Co. of Matthews (9/15/98)

HENSHAW, Mrs. H.P. - of Indianapolis; dt Mrs. Addie Winslow of Fmt. (3/2/99)

HERRINGTON, Silas - funeral was in Pleasant Grove Ch. 14 Jul 1900 (7/19/00)

HESTER, Rev. Jacob - pastor, Fmt. W.M. Ch. (2/7/89); signed charges against Rev. G.P. Riley (8/29/89)

HESTER/[HERTER], George - m Edith Coile of Gas City 23 Aug 1899 (8/31/99)

HETLEY, George - and partners are organizing new Borrey Window Glass Factory (4/29/98)

HIATT, Rev. __ - is holding revival in Jonesboro Friends MH where several people are claiming to be healed although Hiatt is not encouraging it (10/22/97)

HIATT, Eli - of Jonesboro; age 84; d 14 Feb 1898 (2/18/98)

HIATT, Elmer E. - night watchman at Big Four Window Glass Works, while at work accidentally shot himself in the leg with his own revolver while trying to shoot rats (7/9/97); a winner at recent shoot sponsored by Fmt. Gun Club at Fmt. Fair Grounds (10/22/97); s Susannah Hiatt (dec) (9/15/98); helped re-activate Fmt. Gun Club; 20 Sep 1899 won Club Shoot at Fmt. Fair Grounds (9/21/99); a winner in the 3rd shoot of season at Fmt. Gun Club (7/12/00); winner in recent Fmt. Gun Club shoot (9/20/00; 11/1/00)

HIATT, Georgia - of Fmt.; age ca 16 (2/8/00)

HIATT, Jemima - see Eli B. LIGHTFOOT

HIATT, M.A. - owns/operates Hiatt Farm Machinery & Vehicle Store (7/25/89); President, Fmt. Town Board (12/3/97); s Cuthbert Hiatt (6/22/99)

HIATT, Mary E. - dt Susannah Hiatt (dec) (9/15/98)

HIATT, Susannah - age 83; widow; d 11 Sep 1898, bur Buck Creek Cem near Muncie (9/15/98)

HIGHLEY, Mrs. Anne - of Fmt. is dt Mrs. Jennie Mason of Hackleman area (2/12/91)

HIGHLEY, David F. - lives near Pipe Creek in Grant Co.; 21 May 1898 while crossing a bridge over the flooded Pipe Creek, bridge washed away, drowning his horse, destroying his buggy, and dumping he and his wife in the raging creek; his wife's clothing helped her remain afloat until she was deposited in tree branches in the creek; David was able to get out of the water and go for help; at 10:00 PM, he came to Marion Retherford's home asking for help in saving his wife; a crowd gathered and David offered $1,000 for his wife's rescue; after much effort Marion Retherford and William Miller rescued Mrs. Highley; Mr. Highley then refused to pay the $1,000 and rescuers took him to court; a lower court judgement against Highley for $1,000 plus court costs was made; Highley now intends to appeal to the Supreme Court (8/1/00)

HILL, Aaron - prominent early settler in Fmt. Twp. (1/7/92)

HILL. Amanda - see Amanda KNIGHT

HILL, Emilie R. - see Emilie R. SCOTT

HILL, Hannah - see Hannah WILSON

HILL, Sarah - see Thomas W. NEWBY

HIMELICK, John - will teach in Trask Sch 1892-93 (6/2/92)

HINER, Lottie B. - see Edmond H. SEALE

HINKLE, Joe - employed by Long's Store (7/25/89)

HINSHAW, Eleanor - see Eleanor MOON

HIPES, __ - see Mrs. Marion HALL

HIPES, John - owner/operator of Hipes' Meat Market (7/25/89); buys hides and furs (12/12/89)

HILL, Aaron - colored; of Liberty Twp; age ca 65; d last Sunday (2/21/89)

HILL, Charles - of Jonesboro is f mbr Battery H, 3rd Artillery; serv Philippines (11/9/99)

HILL, J.H. - of Jonesboro; helped construct framing for old mill that recently burned in N. Jonesboro (5/29/96)

HILL, S.B. - mgr., Fmt. Telephone Co. (6/3/98); f lived in PA (4/12/00); serves as night and weekend telephone operator (2/15/00); parents live in western PA (5/10/00)

HIMELICK, Robert W. - named as 1896-97 Supt., Fmt. Schs (3/6/96; 4/9/97); att DePauw Univ (6/5/96); 24 Jun 1896 m Rena, dt of L.G. Richards a Delaware Co. farmer; will live in Fmt. (7/3/96)

HINKLE, __ - child of Miles Hinkle; d 27 May 1900 (5/31/00)

HINKLE, Cordia Isabelle - b 18 May 1896; dt Miles and Florence Hinkle; d 10 Aug 1897, bur BC Friends Cem (8/13/97)

HINKLE, Margaret Jane (Nose) - age 40y, 3m, 18da (b 1860); dt George and Sarah Nose; m Joseph Hinkle 1883; d 15 Jul 1900 (7/19/00)

HINKLE, Miles - age ca 55; d 6 Dec 1900 (12/10/00)

HINKLE, Wilber - b 22 Feb 1896; s Joseph and Margaret Jane (Nose); d 26 May 1900 (7/19/00)

HOBBS, Charles M. - Fmt. Twp. Dist. # 7 Sch tchr (12/5/89; 3/19/91); Grant Sch tchr (9/3/91); read scripture at a literary exercise of Fmt. Twp. Schs 1, 4, 6, and 7 held Thanksgiving Day in Bethel P.M. MH (12/1/92); named as 1896-97 Principal, North Bldg. of Fmt. Schs (3/6/96)

HOBBS, Mrs. Charles M. - dt William Duling of Liberty area (6/25/97)

HOBBS, Eva - mbr, Fmt. M.E. Ch. (1/3/96)

HOBBS, Grace B. - grad Fmt. HS 1900 (5/10/00)

HOBSON, Abigail C. (Mendenhall) - b Randolph Co., NC 30 May 1830; m Nathan Hobson (d 1871) in Honey Creek Friends MH 14 Jun 18[54]; Recorded Friends Minister by Honey Creek Friends [of Howard Co.] on [13 Aug] 1867; was a tchr in New London[, Howard Co.]; d 12 Feb 1897 (3/5/97; 2/9/99)

HOBSON, Adella - see Adella LINDLEY

HOBSON, Nathan - m Abigail C. Mendenhall; d 1871 (3/5/97; 2/9/99)

HOCKETT, Mrs. Isaac - Nixon Rush presided over her funeral at BC Friends MH 23 Mar 1896 (3/27/96)

HOCKETT, Josephine - see Silas E. ADDISON

HOCKETT, Lewis - mbr Fmt. Friends boy's SS class (1/11/00)

HOCKETT, Lewis - of Fmt.; to be Supt., White's Training Sch and Orphan's Asylum [White's Institute], near Wabash (4/2/97); m; resigns as Supt., White's Institute (11/5/97)

HOCKETT, Oliver 'Ollie' - 1891 grad of a Liberty Twp. sch (5/21/91); has 50 pupils as Center Sch tchr (10/1/91; 3/31/92); dismissed sch for two weeks for corn husking (11/5/91); had cyphering match at Center Sch last Monday night (12/17/91); 14 Jul 1897 m Ella Haisley (7/16/97)

HOCKETT, Oscar B. - 1898-1900 tchr, Fmt. Twp. Sch No. 7 (Liberty Sch) (3/30/99; 4/12/00); grad FFA 1897 (4/26/00); 1900-01 Grant Sch tchr (11/1/00)

HOCKETT, S.A. - artist who copies and tints pictures (4/14/92)

HOCKETT, Susanna - mbr Oak Ridge WCTU (6/3/98)

HODSON, Aaron/Alfred - m; house was burned by malfunction of natural gas flow in heating/lighting system (1/14/92); filed suit against Fmt. Mining Co. for burning his house, asks $600 damages (1/21/92)

HODSON, Eunice C. (Pitts) - b 10 Nov 1854 Carthage; dt Jessie (dec 1872) and Martha Pitts; m Jessie Hodson 25 Aug 1880; d 10 Nov 1900, bur Marion IOOF Cem (11/15/00)

HODSON, Lawrence - age 1m, 28da; s Aaron and Cynthia A. Hodson; d 28 Aug 1897 (9/3/97)

HODUPP, Herman - of Jonesboro recently d (2/22/00)

HOFFMAN, Emma J. (Reese) - b Fmt. Twp. 20 Sep 1868; dt Rueben and Lydia Jane Reese; m Elwood Hoffman 3 Nov 1889; mbr Friends; d at home of her sister, Ruth A. (Reese) Peacock, 27 Jun 1896, bur Penn, Cass Co., MI (7/3/96)

HOGUE, Fern - of Fmt.; age ca 16 (2/8/00)

HOGUE, Madge - of Fmt.; age ca 16 (2/8/00)

HOLDER, Levi P. - sells fruit trees (5/16/89)

HOLLIDAY, Dr. D.A. - Fmt. physician & surgeon (2/5/97); has moved into property he purchased from William Yaw; is building a barn on his new property (6/18/97); s M/M M.M. Holiday of Losantville (9/29/98)

HOLLIDAY, Mrs. D.A. - is sister of Miss Ida Murray of Henry Co. (12/29/98)

HOLLINGSWORTH, Anna (Brooks) - b OH 23 Aug 1814; dt Nimrod and Elizabeth Brooks; 5 Oct 1834 m Joseph Hollingsworth; came to Grant Co. ca 1837; mbr Friends; d 8 Aug 1897 (8/13/97)

HOLLINGSWORTH, Cyrus - drew up plans for new Fmt. Friends MH (3/19/91); s Joseph and Anna (Brooks) (8/13/97)

HOLLINGSWORTH, Delilah Ann (Carroll) - mbr Fmt. Women's Relief Corps (11/14/89); b Marion 27 Mar 1842; dt Thomas and Ellen

Carroll; 18 Mar 1860 m Wesley B. Hollingsworth; lived in Fmt.; Charter Mbr, Fmt. Congregational Ch.; d 9 Dec 1898 (12/15/98)

HOLLINGSWORTH, Ed - employed in Edwards Drug Store (7/25/89)

HOLLINGSWORTH, Mrs. Eleanor - of Fmt.; age 74; d 30 Aug 1898, bur Gas City Cem (9/2/98)

HOLLINGSWORTH, Elizabeth - see Elizabeth WRIGHT

HOLLINGSWORTH, Gilmore - CW vet bur BC Friends Cem (5/23/89; 6/5/96)

HOLLINGSWORTH, Henry - s Joseph and Anna (Brooks) (8/13/97)

HOLLINGSWORTH, John B. - of Fmt.; CW vet of Co. H, 12th Ind. Regmt.; att party with other Co. H mbrs 6 Jan 1899 (1/12/99)

HOLLINGSWORTH, Joseph - b OH; 1833 came here; m in 1834; had 4 children, 3 sons, 1 dt; mbr Friends; age 74y, 8m, 12 da; d 3 Feb 1889, bur BC Friends Cem (2/7/89; 2/21/89)

HOLLINGSWORTH, Joshua - employed by Flanagan & Henley's Store (7/25/89); s Joseph and Anna (Brooks) (8/13/97)

HOLLINGSWORTH, Linnie - had 15th birthday 9 July 1889 (7/11/89)

HOLLINGSWORTH, Mary (Hall) - has a millinery shop (4/14/92; 3/27/96); dt William Hall; m J. Burgess Hollingsworth (10/11/00)

HOLLINGSWORTH, Mary E. - dt Joseph and Anna (Brooks) Hollingsworth (8/13/97)

HOLLINGSWORTH, Mintie - see Mintie LOTTRIDGE

HOLLINGSWORTH, Sarah J. - see Ezra N. OAKLEY

HOLLINGSWORTH, Wesley B. - Trustee, Fmt. Congregational Ch. (2/10/89); lives in Fmt.; serv Co. K, 130th Regmt. Ind. Vol. Inf. during CW (9/15/92); att his Unit Reunion in Elwood 6 Aug 1896

(8/7/96); 18 Mar 1860 m Delilah Ann Carroll (12/15/98); b Pittsburg, PA 21 May 1834; s William and Lucinda; mbr GAR; d 7 Apr 1900 (4/12/00)

HOLLIS, Mina - Jefferson Twp. Dist. # 5 Sch tchr (2/19/91); - see Ed McCUEN

HOLLOWAY, __ - b 2 Aug 1900; dt M/M Eri Holloway (8/9/00)

HOLLOWAY, Abner - of East Branch area is granted a CW vet pension of $6 per month (9/29/92)

HOLLOWAY, Eleanor (Hinshaw) - see Eleanor MOON

HOLLOWAY, Eri - recently bought license to m Clara Jones of Fmt. Twp. (1/4/00)

HOLLOWAY, Nettie - see Joel LITTLE

HOLLOWELL, Gertrude - see Lem DICKEY

HOOD, James F. - tchr, Pt. Isabel Sch (12/5/89)

HOOD, Wyly - d recently (6/7/00)

HOOVER, Mrs. Amanda - Little Ridge WCTU secretary (6/3/98)

HOOVER, David Y. - granted a soldier's pension of $8 per month (7/4/89); d recently, bur Little Ridge Cem (4/26/00)

HOSIER, Wyly - of Hackleman is Marion Coll student (3/1/00)

HOUSTON, C.M. - of Paulding, OH is new prop. of soon-to-open Drew Hotel, Matthews (1/25/00)

HOWELL, __ - infant of Elsie Howell; bur at Oak Ridge last Thursday (1/22/91)

HOWELL, Mrs. C.J. - of Oak Ridge; dt Dr. Isaac Carey of Marion (12/5/89)

HOWELL, Miss Effie - tchr, Liberty Twp. Dist. # 5 Sch (12/5/89)

HOWELL, Glenn E. - 1898-99 att Purdue Univ Sch of Pharmacy (6/8/99); grad FFA 1898 (1/11/00); 1899-1900 att Ind. Medical Sch, Indianapolis (2/22/00)

HOWELL, Jeremiah 'Jerry'- old resident living near Jonesboro; d 13 Nov 1899 (11/13/89)

HOWELL, Riley - and wife of Hackleman area will celebrate their 50th wedding anniv 7 Oct 1897 (10/1/97)

HOWELL, Mrs. Robert - of Hackleman area, sister of John Levell of Michigan (10/6/92)

HOWELL, Thurza - stockholder in f Farmers and Merchants State Bank (2/22/00)

HOWER, D.I. - Fmt. M.E. Ch. pastor (4/9/97; 6/25/97)

HUGHES, Clarence Albert - b 15 Apr 1892; s M/M Samuel Hughes; d 28 Mar 1899 (3/30/99; 4/6/99)

HUMBARD, Mahala C. - see Mahala C. ARNETT

HUMPHREYS, Elizabeth A. - see Elizabeth A. POWELL

HUNT, John A. - establishes Hunt & Ferree Furniture Store with partner John Ferree (4/10/96); is a funeral director (6/18/97)

HUNT, Mrs. John A. - her father, J.V. Smith of Madison Co. is dec (4/17/96)

HURLESS, W.A. - White House Restaurant prop. (1/11/00)

HUSHAW, Julia A. - see Julia A. LEWIS

HUSHAW, Phoebe (Reed) - b 2 Feb 1826 VA; 1 Jul 1841 m Joseph Hushaw (dec  20 May 1880); mbr M.E. Ch.; d Fmt. 31 Jan 1897, bur Hopewell Ch. Cem, Wabash Co. (2/5/97)

HUTCHINS, Miss Lowie - 1898-99 Little Ridge Sch tchr (1/12/99)

ICE, __ - see Mrs. Joe CORN

ICE, Andy - and brother Ben run Ice & Co. Dry Goods Store (7/25/89)

ICE, Anna Irena - b 17 Feb 1887; d 2 Dec 1897 (12/10/97)

ICE, David O. - s Ransom Ice (8/31/99)

ICE, Mrs. David O. - dt William A. and Margaret Ann (Keith) Brown (6/8/99)

ICE, Oliver - of E of Fmt.; charged with 'cruelty to animals' because he left his driving horse hitched, in harness, to a post in Marion overnight (3/27/96)

ICE, Ransom - age 67; d 25 Aug 1899, bur Harmony Cem (8/31/99)

ICE, Walter - of Fmt.; s William Ice of Leach (3/30/99)

ILIFF, Rev. M.F. - pastor, Jonesboro M.P. Ch. (6/26/96); pastor of Fmt. M.P. Ch. (1/22/97); to give invocation at Bethel for Fmt. Twp. Schs commencement June 11th (6/10/98)

INK, Ida - mbr Fmt. W.M. SS (9/26/89)

JACKSON, Austin - Liberty Twp. District # 8 Sch tchr (2/26/91)

JACKSON, John - of Jonesboro; d 21 Mar 1892 (3/24/92)

JAQUES, F.M. - owns Jaques Clothing Store (3/27/96)

JAY, __ - b 24 Dec 1888; s M/M Elmer Jay (12/27/88)

JAY, Clinton - of Liberty Twp. recently m Leona S. Osborn, a Marion tchr (5/5/92)

JAY, Emma - young dt Riley Jay; d 12 Nov 1889 (11/14/89)

JAY, Ethel - dt M.B. and __ (Carter) Jay (9/22/98)

JAY, Isaiah - donates a 21 volume set of books to the Fmt. Public Library (2/12/97)

JAY, Jesse - mbr BC Friends Cem Improvement Committee (9/1/92)

JAY, Miss Jessie Montese - will be a performer in the 'Holiday Musicale' sponsored by Fmt. IOOF Lodge given in Parker's Opera House 30 Dec 1897 (12/24/97); b Fmt. 6 Aug 1881; dt M.B. and __ (Carter) Jay; FFA senior; grad-Mershon Sch of Music, Marion; violin scholarship student in Cincinnati Coll of Music; mbr Friends (9/22/98); will give violin concert in Fmt.; PHOTO (9/6/00)

JAY, Nettie - Fairmount WCTU mbr (4/2/97)

JAY, Riley - sells his barbershop to Marion Tweedy (10/17/89); barbershop now sold to Daniel Gallimore (11/12/91); recently purchased Lem Pemberton's barbershop; he employs barbers Loman McNeil and Bert Sherwin (7/2/97); is Fmt. Town Marshall (6/5/96); moved his barbershop equipment to Marion (4/15/98)

JAY, Walter L. - local sch tchr; recently returns from a walk through North and South Carolina (7/13/99); 1899-1900 Fmt. HS tchr (8/24/99); mbr/officer Fmt. IOOF (1/4/00); att Ind. Law Sch (12/6/00); 27 Dec 1900 m Geneva Sanders, dt M/M John Sanders of near Matthews (12/31/00)

JAY, William - CW vet bur BC Friends Cem (5/23/89; 6/5/96)

JEAN, Mary L. - see Mary L. WINSLOW

JEFFERSON TOWNSHIP SCHOOLS
DISTRICT # 5 - tchr is Mina Hollis (2/19/91)
DISTRICT # 10 - 1891-92 tchr is Alvin Dickerson (3/31/92)
TRASK SCHOOL - John Himelick to be 1892-93 tchr (6/2/92)

JEFFREY, Glenn Aldine - s Henry R. Jeffrey, d 21 Apr 1889, bur Park Cem (4/25/89)

JESSUP, __ - see Mrs. S.C. WILSON

JESSUP, J.C. - b Guilford Co., NC 9 Jan 1842; s Joseph B. and Mary Jessup; 1873 m Hannah Cox in Fairfield, IA; 1894 moved to Fmt. from Marshall Co., IA; d 9 Jun 1900, bur Park Cem (6/14/00; 6/21/00)

JESSUP, Thomas - of Rush Co.; father of Mrs. S.C. Wilson; d 7 Apr 1892 (4/14/92)

JOHNSON, infant - child M/M Frank Johnson; d 28 Aug 1900 (8/30/00)

JOHNSON, Mr. __ - 1899-1900 tchr, Little Ridge Sch, Liberty Twp. (10/19/99)

JOHNSON, Albert H. - f Fmt. Postmaster; d 15 Dec 1891 in LaGrange, KY where he was a businessman (1/7/92)

JOHNSON, Barclay - and wife leave next wk for Southland Coll, Helena, Arkansas where he will be Supt. and she will be Matron of this Friends Teachers Coll for colored people; the Coll owns 120 acres where students raise food for Coll (10/5/99)

JOHNSON, Bertha May (Coggeshall) - dt M/M Eli Coggeshall; m Ernest V. Johnson 22 Jul 1896 (8/12/98; 8/19/98)

JOHNSON, Calvin C. - and Charles E. and Elva are children Gabriel and Ursula (Coppock) Johnson (6/21/00)

JOHNSON, Ernest V. - age 25; s Barclay and S. Anna; m Bertha May Coggeshall 22 Jul 1896; father of Zora Pauline and of Ernest; grad-FFA; taught sch several yr; d 9 Aug 1898, bur Park Cem (8/12/98; 8/19/98)

JOHNSON, Gabriel 'Gabe' - employee, Latham's Harness Shop (7/25/89); officer, Beeson Post of GAR (12/10/91); prominent early settler in Fmt. Twp. (1/7/92); 19 Jan 1896 is given party for his 59th birthday (1/24/96); mbr Fmt. Sch Board (6/15/99); mbr/officer Fmt. IOOF (1/4/00); b Grant Co. 19 Jan 1837; m 1st 9 Sep 1866 Julia A. Shelton at Hartford City; moved to IL 1869, wife d there in 1870; moved to Jonesboro in 1871; m Ursula Coppock 1874; moved to Fmt. 1878; was a carpenter until CW; enlisted 28 Aug 1861 in Co. A, 8th Ind. Regmt.; discharged 4 Sep 1864; was harness maker since CW; mbr Fmt. Congregational Ch.; mbr GAR; d 14 Jun 1900, bur Park Cem (6/14/00; 6/21/00)

JOHNSON, H.E. - mgr., Crystal Ice Plant (8/9/00)

JOHNSON, H.M. - Fmt. M.E. Ch. pastor (4/10/96)

JOHNSON, James - in 1893 was a stockholder in Farmers and Merchants Bank (2/22/00)

JOHNSON, Jesse - Upland banker; assaulted recently by Jesse Ferguson, one of his tenants (1/29/97)

JOHNSON, Lafe - shot and wounded by John Hefren, Jonesboro tailor, while both were drunk (7/25/89)

JOHNSON, Lucy - of Jonesboro; widow of Dr. Joseph Johnson (dec ca 1886); d last Sunday (3/11/98)

JOHNSON, Miss Nettie - is substituting as Little Ridge Sch tchr (2/8/00)

JOHNSON, Nettie Maude - see Nettie Maude WINSLOW

JOHNSON, Noah - age 22; s John F. Johnson of 3.5 mi. N of Upland; in fit of jealousy last wk shot Tacie Mang, age 17, dt Martin Mang of 4 mi. N of Upland; she d instantly (10/1/97); is sentenced to life in prison (1/21/98)

JOHNSON, Reuben - of Fmt.; d 7 May 1900, bur Park Cem (5/10/00)

JOHNSON, Ursula (Coppock) - dt Calvin Coppock (9/15/98)

JONES, __ - b 30 Aug 1892; s M/M Lewis Jones (9/1/92)

JONES, Abijah - of Jonesboro d last Friday (6/6/89)

JONES, Burr - s J.W. Jones (1/21/98)

JONES, Charles - of Jonesboro; during CW serv Co. C, 7th Ind. Cav. (10/12/99)

JONES, Clara - see Eri HOLLOWAY

JONES, Clayton - 'White Egg' Sch tchr (12/5/89); pupils are colored (12/19/89)

JONES, Miss Dollie - of Liberty area was given party 1 Jul 1897 for her 21st birthday (7/2/97)

JONES, Frank - CW vet of Co. H, 12th Ind. Regmt.; att party with other Co. H mbrs 6 Jan 1899 (1/12/99)

JONES, Mrs. Hannah - see Jesse WRIGHT

JONES, Henry - employee, Dillon Glass Works (9/24/91)

JONES, Hiram A. - a gas well is being drilled on his farm; att GAR encampment in Washington, D.C.; had his daughter's wedding to Elwood Rich in his home (10/13/92)

JONES, J.W. - East Branch Sch tchr (11/21/89; 12/5/89); 1895-96 tchr, Orestes Sch (4/10/96); d 13 Jan 1898, bur Park Cem (1/21/98)

JONES, James P. - teaches in Liberty Twp Sch #12 during absence of tchr, J.D. Latham (1/10/89); finishes term at Liberty Twp Sch # 3 because of the death of tchr, Silas L. Becks (2/21/89); b Apr 1862 in Wabash Co.; began teaching in Huntington Co. in 1882; tchr, Crane Pond Sch in Van Buren Twp., Grant Co. in 1883; m Myrtle Kimes of Liberty Twp. 1888; is Principal of Woodland, IL Schs (10/3/89)

JONES, Jennie W. - mbr Fmt. Women's Relief Corps (11/14/89)

JONES, John - of OH; s Susan Bailey (dec) (8/6/97)

JONES, John F. - officer, Beeson Post, GAR (12/10/91)

JONES, Maria (Miller) - m; sister of Hezekiah Miller and of Isaiah Miller (7/28/92); of Hackleman area is having several gas wells drilled on her farm (3/30/99)

JONES, Nettie - see Nettie RICH

JONES, Sallie - mbr Fmt. Women's Relief Corps (11/14/89)

JONES, Thed - mbr Fmt. Friends boy's SS class (1/11/00)

JONES, Thomas - works in back room of Eagle Shoe Store (7/25/89); officer, Beeson Post, GAR (12/10/91); dec; s Sarah Bailey (dec) (8/6/97)

JONES, Willie - to grad 9 Jun 1899 from Fmt. Twp. Schs (6/1/99)

JONES, Z.M. - CW vet bur in Park Cem (6/5/96)

JONESBORO, Town of - old flour mill in North Jonesboro burned 22 May 1896 with a loss of $6,000; J.H. Hill of Jonesboro helped build framing for this old mill (5/29/96)
METZLER FRUIT JAR WORKS - is being built (11/26/91)

KEARNS, Mary (Stuart) - b NC; age 63y, 8m, 3da; dt Jehu and Rebecca Stuart; 1850 m Thomas Kearns; mbr Friends; d 20 Nov 1891(12/3/91)

KEELY, Dolly - runs Keely Boarding House (10/26/99)

KEENER, __ - see Mrs. John DENNIS

KEEVER, Cleo - b 12 Apr 1892; dt William and Ella Keever; d 4 Jul 1898 (7/15/98)

KEITH, Margaret Ann - see Margaret Ann BROWN

KELLY, Jane - see Jane HARVEY

KELSAY, Adin - mbr Fmt. Friends boy's SS class (1/11/00)

KELSAY, Albert - landholder advertising 'no hunting' on his property (10/13/92)

KELSAY, Charles - 20 Feb 1897 m Luella Lane; will live in Fmt. (2/26/97)

KELSEY, Guy - att Purdue Univ (9/17/97; 6/10/98); s John Kelsay; grad Purdue Univ 1900 in electrical engineering (6/7/00)

KELSAY, John - Fmt. Twp. Trustee (10/6/92)

KELSAY, Luella (Lane) - b 25 Dec 1876; dt John and Lois Lane (both dec); 20 Feb 1897 m Charles Kelsay; d 8 Oct 1899 (10/12/99)

KELSAY, Rust - of Fmt.; CW vet of Co. H, 12th Ind. Regmt.; att party with other Co. H mbrs 6 Jan 1899 (1/12/99)

KELSEY, Sarah - see W.D. MONTGOMERY

KELSAY, Verlie - age 16 months; s Charles and Luella (Lane) Kelsay (10/12/99)

KENNEDY, Ella - see Arthur E. SEALE

KENNEDY, J.R. - left for KS last wk to help thresh wheat (6/28/00)

KENNEDY, W.H. - acted for Ind. Conference of W.M. Ch. in bringing charges against Rev. G.P. Riley (8/29/89)

KEPLER, __ - b 22 Sep 1892; s M/M H. Lewis Kepler (9/22/92); d 27 Sep 1892 (9/29/92)

KEPLER, H. Lewis - is a jeweler in Edwards Drug Store (7/25/89; 4/14/92); m; has party for his 27th birthday 28 Sept 1891 (10/1/91); now tests eyes and sells glasses (8/11/92); moved to Andrews in Huntington Co. 4 yr ago; b Marion Co., OH 28 Sep 1865; s M/M Henry Kepler of Fmt.; m Cora L. Trott 9 Jun 1888; mbr M.E. Ch.; d 29 Dec 1897, bur Park Cem (12/31/97; 1/7/98)

KEPLER, Mrs. H. Lewis - dt Mrs. Elcie Trott of Howard Co. (7/14/92)

KEPLER, Hazel Inez - b 28 Mar 1889; dt M/M H. Lewis Kepler (4/4/89); d 7 Jul 1892, bur Park Cem (7/14/92)

KEPLER, Henry - his CW pension is increased from $6 per month to $12 per month (7/12/00)

KESTER, Ella - mbr United Brethren Ch. (4/16/97)

KEY, Sol - is a barber in Fowlerton (3/12/97)

KIBBEY, John E. - s Jonah Kibbey (1/28/92)

KIBBEY, Jonah - lived 2.5 mi. N of New Cumberland; recently dec (1/28/92)

KILGORE, Estin I. - age 22; m; d 21 Jun 1896 at his Green Twp. home of a kick by a horse, bur Knox Chapel Cem (6/26/96)

KILLEN, Ruth - see Milton GOSSETT

KIMBROUGH, __ - baby of M/M Will Kimbrough d 18 July 1889, bur BC Friends Cem (7/25/89)

KIMES, Benjamin F. - 15 Dec 1897 m Carrie A. Ringo, both are from Hackleman area (12/24/97)

KIMES, Ed L. - mbr, Fmt. Gun Club (9/21/99); a winner in 3rd shoot of season at Fmt. Gun Club (7/12/00); a winner in Fmt. Gun Club shoot last Mon. PM (9/20/00)

KIMES, Jennie Pearl (Sullivan) - b Rush Co. 6 Oct 1877; dt John L. and Nancy Ann Sullivan; came to Grant Co. 1879; m Charles R. Kimes 10 Nov 1894; lived 5 mi. SW of Fmt.; d 17 May 1900 (5/24/00)

KIMES, M. - mbr/officer Fmt. IOOF (1/4/00)

KIMES, Mabel Marie - b 4 Aug 1897; dt M/M Charles Kimes; d 19 Feb 1899 (2/23/99)

KIMES, Marshall - aged man; bur Park Cem last Sun. (10/22/91)

KIMES, Myrtle - see James P. JONES

KIMES, Thomas Grant - b 2 Mar 1862 Montgomery Co., KY; s Marshall E. and Margaret Jane; d 15 Sep 1897 (9/24/97)

KING, Samuel F. - age 59; of Liberty Twp. d 31 Mar 1900 (4/5/00)

KIRK, Mrs. John - of Trask; is dt M/M Joseph Weimer of Wabash (6/2/92)

KIRKLAND, Sophronia - see Willard Emory FELLOWS

KIRKWOOD, Mrs. Frank - d 2 Mar 1889, bur BC Friends Cem (3/7/89)

KIRKWOOD, John D. - in 1893 was a stockholder in Farmers and Merchants Bank (2/22/00)

KIRSCHBAUM, B. - recently established One Price Clothing House (4/14/92)

KITTERMAN, Zellous Grace - b 3 Jun 1896; dt Ennis and Phebe Kitterman; d 10 Aug 1897, bur Park Cem (8/20/97)

KLEESPIES, Lewis - applies for license to retail liquors in Fmt. (11/24/92); operates a Fmt. saloon (6/25/97)

KNIGHT, __ - b 3 Nov 1889; dt M/M R.P. Knight (11/7/89)

KNIGHT, __ - age 8 yr; s M/M Thomas Knight; d 29 Dec 1898, bur Pendleton cem (1/5/99)

KNIGHT, Albert D. - grad Fmt. HS 1900 (5/10/00)

KNIGHT, Amanda (Hill) - b 5 Feb 1862; dt Nathan and Emeline Hill; m Charles E. Knight 29 Sep 1878; mbr Friends; d 11 Oct 1898 (10/13/98)

KNIGHT, Charles - f of Fmt., now of Jonesboro; s Thomas Knight; 30 Jul 1897 drowned in Yellow Lake, Kosciusko Co. (8/6/97)

KNIGHT, Charles - recently m Ida Harvey (10/19/99)

KNIGHT, Josephine - dt Charles E. And Amanda (Hill) Knight (10/13/98)

KNIGHT, Shell - is a Fmt. house painter (7/9/97); husband of Lutie (11/19/97); brother of Steve Knight of New York City (9/28/99)

KNIGHT, Solomon - prominent early settler in Fmt. Twp. (1/7/92)

KNIGHT, Steve - brother of Shell Knight (12/27/88)

KNIGHT, Thomas W. - of Fmt.; will open an undertaking establishment in Jonesboro (9/29/92)

KNIGHT, William Merle - b Chicago, IL 8 Nov 1890; s Shell W. and Lutie Knight; brother of Garr Knight; d 11 Nov 1897, bur Park Cem (11/12/97; 11/19/97)

KNOOB, Jacob - f Fmt. saloonkeeper; m; is in Marion jail at his own request; he may be insane (4/13/99)

KNUCK, Ed - manufactures cigars in his Fmt. home (10/13/92)

LAKE GALATIA - 4th of July celebration will be held here with an oration by A.L. Reynolds of Ohio (6/20/89); Hen Gillispie recently killed a black rattlesnake near here (7/2/91); it is proposed to ditch the lake into Barren Creek (11/17/92); located 3.5 mi. E of Fmt.; A.M. Baldwin plans to make a summer resort here, will have rowboats, a steam launch and a small hotel (5/25/97)

LAMB, Nona Belle - b Grant Co. 14 Aug 1887; dt William and Cordie; mbr Fmt. Baptist Ch.; d 25 Aug 1900 (8/30/00; 9/6/00)

LANE, Luella - see Charles KELSAY

LANE, Lydia - see Francis M. VERNON

LaPORTE, Orpha - see Charles S. BRILES

LARKINS, Moses - of Summitville; f of Fmt.; age 83; d recently (9/22/98)

LaRUE, __ - b 19 Oct 1991; s M/M Gilbert LaRue (10/29/91)

LaRUE, Gilbert 'Gib' - hunted rabbits with Millard Clark and Bob Ray last Friday (12/5/89); & Co. owns Planing Mill & Excelsior Firm, employs 25 persons and ships 4 carloads of product each wk (7/30/91); b Franklin Co. (4/14/92); and others petition the county to construct a ditch to be known as 'Whybrew & Flanagan Ditch' (2/26/97); granted franchise by Fmt. Town Board to construct electric light plant (11/12/97); offers to sell his electric light plant to City of Fmt. so electric street lights may be installed

(9/15/98); has reached agreement with the town on their securing his electric light plant (12/1/98)

LaRUE, Lonnie - works in Cook's Grocery (8/16/00)

LaRUE, Will - m Catherine Troy 1 Sep 1900 (9/6/00)

LASTERS, Sallie - lives with her aunt, Mrs. Sallie Frazier; is given surprise party for her 16th birthday 11 Jan 1889 (1/17/89)

LATHAM, Ione - see Dr. C.B. VIGUS

LATHAM, Joseph D. - is replaced by J.P. Jones as Liberty Twp Sch #12 tchr (1/10/89); replaces his father, T.P. Latham, as Fmt. Postmaster (5/30/89)

LATHAM, Mrs. Joseph D. - of Fmt. is dt Mrs. J.A. Maddy of Muncie (3/26/91)

LATHAM, Miss Myrtle - Deputy Postmaster (7/25/89)

LATHAM, T.P. - resigns as Fmt. Postmaster (5/30/89); Fmt. businessman (8/8/89); b VA 20 Oct 1832; came to Fmt. ca 1881; owns harness & buggy shop (4/14/92); b Apr 1832 Hopewell, Faulkner Co., VA; 1857 m Syna M. Duling in OH; 1881 came to Fmt.; mbr M.P. Ch.; was Fmt. Postmaster for 4 yr; d 16 Oct 1897 (10/22/97)

LAWRENCE, India - has a dressmaking shop on Penn St. with her sister, Mrs. Jacob Briles (8/24/99)

LAWRENCE, Thomas H. - b Randolph Co., NC 9 Mar 1825; m Grant Co. 23 Oct 1850 Ann Marie Cox; mbr Friends; d 28 Jan 1892, bur New Garden Cem, Fountain City (2/4/92)

LAY, James A. - granted a CW pension of $12 per month (6/25/91)

LEACH, Audie - see Otto PICKARD

LEACH, Esom, Sr. - d 16 Jan 1889, bur Harmony Baptist Cem (1/17/89; 1/24/89)

LEACH, Esom, Jr. - is a gas well driller (10/31/89)

LEACH, Esom O. - Deputy Marshall for Fmt. (6/5/96); has patented and is selling the 'Leach Mould Sanding Machine'; picture and description in this issue (1/29/97); hopes to start for Alaska gold fields by mid-February (1/28/98); and son Noah hope to start to Alaska as soon as The Klondyke Mining Co, Fmt. raises enough capital at $25 per share (3/4/98); has returned from La Gloria, Cuba where he accompanied 200 Indiana people who wished to set up a colony; he was one of 60 who gave up and returned home (2/1/00); has bought and will operate White House Restaurant (2/15/00)

LEACH, Mrs. George - see Luther HARRISON

LEACH, J.W. - is V. President, Citizen's Exchange Bank (3/20/96)

LEACH, Mary E. - see Mary E. McCOY

LEACH, Mary J. 'Polly' (Lewis) - b Franklin Co. 26 Nov 1829; dt David and Nancy Lewis; 1847 m John Leach (dec); lived E of Fmt.; mbr M.E. Ch.; d 20 Jul 1891, bur Park Cem (7/23/91; 8/13/91)

LEACH, Noah - s Esom O. Leach (3/4/98); has resigned from Big Four Window Glass Factory to go to Alaska gold fields with his father (3/11/98)

LEACH, William - prominent early settler in Fmt. Twp. (1/7/92)

LEACH, William J. - landholder advertising 'no hunting' on his property (10/13/92); donates 15 acres as site of new Fowlerton glass factory (4/17/96)

LEACH, Willie - age 12 yr; dt M/M E.O. Leach; d 15 Oct 1900, bur Park Cem (10/18/00)

LEAVELLE, Lydia J. - see Lydia J. TAYLOR

LEDBETTER, Sallie - see Jasper N. WHEELER

LEER, Daniel - aged pioneer of near Hackleman; d 23 Sep 1899, bur Knox Chapel Cem (9/28/99)

LEER, Miss Lizzie - d 28 May 1892 at Hackleman (6/2/92)

LEER, Mrs. Sam - of Hackleman area; m; d 7 May 1891, bur Knox Chapel Cem (5/14/91)

LEES, __ - 1 yr old child of M/M Harmon Lees of Hackleman area; d recently (6/26/96)

LEMON, Isaac F. - purchased Big Four Restaurant from Perry Woods (6/7/00)

LEMON, J. Marion - owns Fmt. fruit market (4/14/92)

LERVISE, Lee - landholder advertising 'no hunting' on his property (10/13/92)

LEVELL, __ - see Mrs. Robert HOWELL

LEWIS, __ - child of M/M Oliver Lewis; d 29 Dec 1900 (12/31/00)

LEWIS, Carl - is Asst. Clerk, Northern Indiana Penitentiary (7/12/00)

LEWIS, Clyde - s Mrs. Ed Lewis (1/26/99)

LEWIS, Goldie - age 19; dt Edward D. Lewis; is suing Morton Buller for rape and for fathering her child b 3 Jul 1900 (10/11/00)

LEWIS, J.S.D. - CW vet bur BC Friends Cem (5/23/89; 6/5/96)

LEWIS, John R. - age 80; Grant Co. pioneer; d 13 Jan 1896 at his home near Sweetser (1/17/96)

LEWIS, Julia A. (Hushaw) - lives in Fmt.; dt Joseph and Phoebe (Reed) Hushaw (both dec); m Ed Lewis (2/5/97)

LEWIS, Mrs. L.L. - of Fmt. is dt Mrs. Celia Wright of Brookville (11/7/89)

LEWIS, Mary J. - see Mary J. LEACH

LEWIS, Rachel - Fmt. WCTU mbr (4/2/97)

LEWIS, Rebecca A. - see Madison Matthew HAYNES

LEWIS, Mrs. Sarah - of Matthews; grandmother of f Fmt. Chief of Police Carl Lewis; d 11 Jun 1900 (6/14/00)

LIBERTY TOWNSHIP - a new town located on the William S. Elliott farm and on the C.I.&E. RR may be named El Morro (9/15/98); Dr. I.N. Seale resigns as Twp. Trustee; Dennis Haisley is named to replace him (9/22/98)

LIBERTY TOWNSHIP SCHOOLS - 17 Jun 1899 graduation to be held in Oak Ridge Friends MH (6/15/99)
DISTRICT # 1 (BETHEL) - tchr, Mr. Overman of Marion (12/5/89)
DISTRICT # 2 (OAK RIDGE) - Sylvester Haisley, tchr (12/5/89); Will Sherwin (dec) taught here in the past (1/1/91); term closed 5 Mar 1891 (3/12/91); 1891-92 tchr, Charles S. Briles (3/24/92); Will Young, 1895-96 tchr (3/6/96); Miss Ollie Rittenhouse won 1st honors at 1899 graduation (6/22/99)
DISTRICT # 3 (LITTLE RIDGE) - Silas L. Becks, tchr, d 11 Jan 1889; J.P. Jones will teach rest of term (2/21/89); sch house burned down 18 Jan 1892 due to a defective flu (1/21/92); Twp. Trustee Frank Albert signed contracts for new sch bldg.: Al Smith, carpenter; El. Gossett, stone work; and Goodall Bros., brick work (3/24/92); 1892-93 tchrs: William Young and Nettie McMaster (8/25/92); sch bldg. nears completion (9/29/92); 1897-98 tchr is Miss Flo Wells (6/25/97); 1897-98 tchr is Frank McCabe (12/31/97); 1898-99 tchr is Miss Lowie Hutchins (1/12/99); 1899-1900 tchr is Mr. __ Johnson (10/19/99); students include Gertie A. and Orpha E. Bradford (11/16/99); Miss Nettie Johnson is substituting as tchr (2/8/00)
HOWELL SCH - tchr Frank P. McCoy closed term last wk (3/17/92)
DISTRICT # 5 (CENTER) - Miss Effie Howell, tchr (12/5/89); tchr Oliver Hockett has 50 pupils (10/1/91); tchr Hockett dis-missed sch for two weeks for corn husking (11/5/91); cyphering match here last Monday night (12/17/91); Albert Collins, tchr 1892-93 (9/1/92)
PANSY SCH - Charles S. Briles, tchr 1892-93 (8/25/92); C.S. Briles resigns and is replaced by Mr. Floyd from Clinton Co. (10/13/92); Mr. __ Wilson is tchr (10/19/99)

LIBERTY TOWNSHIP SCHOOLS (continued)
DISTRICT # 7 (WEAVER, colored sch) - Miss Asenath Peters and J.W. White, tchrs (12/5/89)
DISTRICT # 8 (ANTIOCH) - Austin Jackson, tchr (2/26/91)
DISTRICT # 9 (RIGDON) - James Sheedy, tchr (12/5/89); Clare McTurnan won 2nd honors at 1899 graduation (6/22/99)
DISTRICT # 10 - Frank P. McCoy, tchr; has over 30 pupils (12/5/89), and is still tchr (3/12/91)
DISTRICT # 11 (WELLS) - new sch bldg. has 50 pupils; C.A. Luse, tchr (12/5/89)
DISTRICT # 12 - J.P. Jones is tchr during absence of tchr J.D. Latham (1/10/89); Miss Louie Rush, tchr (4/4/89)
DISTRICT # 13 (WHITE EGG) - Clayton Jones, tchr (12/5/89); pupils are colored (12/19/89); Friends hold church services in sch house (1/15/91)

LIFE, Andrew - 1897-98 att DePauw Univ (6/3/98)

LIFE, Andrew C. - of Fmt. is 1896 grad of Indiana Univ (6/26/96)

LIFE, Frank - 1896 DePauw Univ grad (5/29/96)

LIFE, Margaret - Fmt. M.E. Ch. mbr (1/3/96)

LIFE, Minta - 1899-1900 Fmt. Elementary Sch tchr (8/24/99)

LIGHTFOOT, Eli B. - b Rush Co. 16 Jan 1834; m Jemima Hiatt 25 Dec 1864; CW vet; d Fmt. 20 Jul 1899 (7/27/99; 8/17/99)

LILLIBRIDGE, John - CW vet bur in Park Cem (6/5/96)

LINDLEY, Adella (Hobson) - dt Nathan and Abigail C. (Mendenhall) Hobson; m (3/5/97); Fmt. WCTU mbr (4/2/97); b near New London 19 Mar 1855; m Gurney Lindley 18 Sep 1890; mbr Friends; lived 2 mi. SW of Fmt.; d 26 Jan 1899, bur New London, Howard Co. (2/2/99; 2/9/99)

LINDLEY, Mrs. Achsah W. - 10 Nov 1898 celebrated her 64th birthday (11/10/98)

LINDLEY, Dwight - mbr Fmt. Friends boy's SS class (1/11/00)

LINDLEY, Maggie - named as 1896-97 Fmt. Schs 2nd grade tchr (3/6/96); 1899-1900 Fmt. Elementary Sch tchr (8/24/99)

LINDLEY, Margaret - see Edward OVERMAN

LINDLEY, Mary - att Earlham Coll (12/20/00)

LINDSEY, William H. - Fmt. Congregational Ch. bldg. committee mbr (12/19/89); employs 10 men in his Fmt. Lumber Mill (4/14/92); 5 Oct 1897 is granted a franchise for an electric plant by Fmt. Town Board (10/8/97); his sawmill burned; he is rebuilding it (6/7/00)

LITTLE CREEK DITCH - in Hackleman area; is being dug deeper and wider (5/17/00)

LITTLE, Alexander - Commander, Beeson Post, GAR (3/21/89); repaired burst connector on gas well just N of BC Friends MH (2/11/92); came to Fmt. area in 1853; has a plumbing shop (4/14/92); CW vet of Co. H, 12th Ind. Regmt.; att party with other Co. H mbrs 6 Jan 1899 (1/12/99); during CW serv Co. B, 7th Ind. Cav. (10/3/89; 10/12/99)

LITTLE, Mrs. Alexander - 25 May 1889 is given party for her birthday (5/23/89)

LITTLE, Annie - dt Thomas and Susanna Little; d recently (8/26/98)

LITTLE, Azeal G. - CW vet bur BC Friends Cem (5/23/89; 6/5/96)

LITTLE, Elizabeth Jane - see Elizabeth Jane WINSLOW

LITTLE, Hattie - see Hattie WALKER

LITTLE, Joel - b 28 Jul 1848 Randolph Co., NC; s John and Rachel; 1853 came to Fmt. area; 1 Feb 1871 m 1st Sarepta McCormick (dec ca 1887); 13 Jun 1890 m 2nd Nettie Holloway; mbr Friends; lived 2.5 mi. E of Fmt.; d 4 Aug 1898, bur Park Cem (8/12/98; 8/26/98)

LITTLE, John - 1900-01 Leachburg Sch tchr; will be his 7th yr there (8/30/00)

LITTLE, Mandy - mbr Fmt. Women's Relief Corps (11/14/89)

LITTLE, Manie - mbr Fmt. Women's Relief Corps (11/14/89)

LITTLE, Mary - see Charles L. MAIN

LITTLE, Nathan - b NC 18 Dec 1814; came to Fmt. Twp. In 1852; lives with his grand-dt, Mrs. Winfield Crisco 2 mi. E of Fmt.; is given party for his 84th birthday (12/22/98)

LITTLE, Rachel (Modlin) - b Wayne Co., NC in Nov 1818; dt John and Nancy Modlin; Oct 1838 m John Little (dec 1853); m 2nd 1859 James Fouse (dec 1876); m 3rd Nathan Little in 1883; d 20 Jan 1898 (1/21/98; 1/28/98)

LITTLE, Thomas - of Fmt.; during CW serv Co. B, 7th Ind. Inf. (10/12/99)

LITTLE, Zack - CW vet bur in Park Cem (6/5/96)

LIVESY/LIVSKY, J. - replaces Frank Sherwin as East Branch Sch tchr (1/8/91; 3/19/91)

LONG, __ - b 7 Jan 1889; s M/M A.R. Long (1/10/89)

LONG, A.R. - owns/operates Long's Store (7/25/89); is new Fmt. Justice of Peace (6/9/92)

LONG, Miss Etta - dt Mrs. Fred Norton, Sr. (10/26/99); - see J.H. WILSON

LONG, J.C. - m Maggie Fouse last Saturday (12/27/88)

LONG, John - age 27; m 20 Aug 1898 killed by train in Jonesboro, bur Jonesboro IOOF Cem (8/26/98)

LONG, Sam - Chinaman who has a hand laundry on W. Washington St. (9/22/98)

LOTTRIDGE, __ - b 10 Jan 1889; dt M/M Frank Lottridge (1/17/89)

LOTTRIDGE, Edith - 28 Jul 1891 given party for her 5th birthday (7/30/91)

LOTTRIDGE, Frank - works for Elmer Flint blacksmith shop (12/27/88); is working as a blacksmith in Hackleman (4/25/89); of Fmt.; m; s M/M Frank Lottridge of Jonesboro (7/4/89)

LOTTRIDGE, Mintie (Hollingsworth) - m; dt Wesley B. And Delilah Ann (Carroll) Hollingsworth (12/15/98); - see Minta SCOTT

LOUTZENHISER, A.B. - sells Central Hotel to Cyrus Roose (10/22/91)

LOWE, Joseph - 21 May 1889 is given party for his 48th birthday (5/23/89)

LOWMAN, Dr. J.O. - is Fmt. Health Officer (5/14/91)

LOWNEY, Dot - see John L. PAYNE

LOY, Mary Opal - b 23 Oct 1896; dt Oscar and Rena Loy; d 15 Jul 1897, bur Park Cem (7/23/97)

LUCAS, Carl - att Ind. Dental Coll (2/22/00; 9/20/00)

LUCAS, Mabel - given party for 16th birthday 7 Nov 1900 (11/15/00)

LUCAS, T.J. - and Elwood Davis own/operate the f C.R. Small Hardware (4/14/92)

LUCAS, Wilbur - att Indiana Medical Coll, Indianapolis (9/21/99; 4/12/00)

LUSE, C.A. - Liberty Twp. Wells Sch tchr (12/5/89)

LUSE, Elmina Clementine - b Grant Co. 31 May 1889; dt Walter and Elmina Luce; d 29 Nov 1898 (12/1/98)

LUTHER, __ - b 19 July 1889; dt M/M James Luther (7/25/89)

LUTHER, Miss Dorothy 'Dorrie' E. - to teach in FFA in f position of J. Marcus Dickey (9/26/89); b NC; moved to Henry Co., att Henry Co. sch taught by Micajah Butler; moved to Grant Co.; in 1881 grad from sch, att Earlham Coll 1 yr; grad Knightstown HS; att summer Normals at Marion; taught Pike Sch (1 term) and Mississinewa Sch near Marion (1 term); 1884 att World Exposition in New Orleans; FFA tchr 1887-88 and at present (11/21/89); to be 1896-97 Fmt. Schs 8th grade tchr (3/6/96); sister of Mrs. Alvin Scott of Fmt. (4/3/96); 1899-1900 Fmt. Grammer Sch tchr (8/24/99)

LUTHER, Emma - see Emma SCOTT

LUTHER, Ivy - his wife is dt of John and Rebecca Stuart (both dec) (9/19/89)

LUTHER, James - employed in Fmt. Bank (7/25/89); Asst. Cashier of Farmer's and Merchant's Bank (8/6/91;11/5/91)

LYNCH, J.M. - mgr., Columbia Hotel (12/29/98); has leased Mississinewa Hotel in Gas City (1/12/99)

LYON, Mrs. Sarah - treasurer of Matthews WCTU (11/10/98)

LYONS, Charles C. - a Fmt. tailor (4/14/92); and Frank B. Zeigler have gone to inspect Hoosier Mining Co. in the Florida Mts. of Idaho in which they own stock (7/20/99)

LYONS, Gladys - 22 Mar 1900 was given party for her 16th birthday (3/29/00)

LYTLE, Mary - see Lindsey BULLER

McCABE, Frank - home is in southern Indiana; is Little Ridge Sch tchr (12/31/97); is new Hackleman postmaster (1/26/99)

McCANDLISS, Richard - and wife have opened a new restaurant in Fmt. (7/7/92); goes into meat business in Indianapolis with Isaac N. Gossett (5/8/96)

McCASKI, H.M. - lives at Rigdon; serv in Co. K, 130th Regmt. Ind. Vol. Inf. during CW (9/15/92)

McCOMBS, __ - b 9 Jan 1899; 8 lb. s M/M John T. McCombs of Hackleman area (1/12/99)

McCOMBS, John T. - of Hackleman area; m 22 Dec 1889 Lizzie Brookshire (12/26/89); recently killed 45 quail with 3 shots (12/25/90)

McCOMBS, Milton - 11 Aug 1892 m Mattie Wood (8/18/92)

McCONNELL, Zoe - age ca 16; of Fmt. (2/8/00)

McCORMICK, Robert - one of first Fmt. Township settlers; purchased land from US Government at the crossing of the Muncie and Indianapolis and Fort Wayne State Roads on 15 Aug 1829 (1/7/92)

McCORMICK, Sarepta - see Joel LITTLE

McCOY, Ann (Moon) - b Clinton Co., OH 13 Sep 1830; dt Thomas and Elizabeth Moon; 2 Jun 1846 m William H. McCoy (d 16 Jun 1893); moved to Oak Ridge in spring 1858; mbr Oak Ridge Friends; d 2 Aug 1899 (8/10/99)

McCOY, Frank P. - tchr, Liberty Twp. Dist. # 10 Sch 1889-91 (12/5/89; 3/12/91); closed Howell Sch term last wk (3/17/92); found guilty in Marion J.P. Court of mistreating student Milton Gibson (4/21/92)

McCOY, Fred - b 22 July 1889; s Robert A. and Ella McCoy; d 30 Oct 1889 in Detroit, MI (7/25/89; 11/7/89)

McCOY, Henry - CW vet bur in Park Cem (6/5/96)

McCOY, Jacob - CW vet bur BC Friends Cem (5/23/89; 6/5/96)

McCOY, Mary E. (Leach) - lived 1 mi. E of Fmt.; b 15 Oct 1854; dt John and Mary Leach (both dec); m Willis McCoy in 1874; mbr Methodist Ch.; d 31 May 1896 (6/5/96)

McCOY, Zola Estella - age 3y, 3m, 14da; dt M/M R.A. McCoy; d 28 Sept 1889 (10/3/89)

McCUEN, Ed - 8 Apr 1891 m Mina Hollis (4/16/91)

McCUNE, Minnie Amanda - b Adams Co. 14 Feb 1858; dt John and Mary McCune (both dec); d 13 Jun 1897, bur Adams Co. (6/18/97)

McDONALD, Rachel J. (Schooley) - b Wayne Co. 14 Oct 1824; dt M/M John Schooley; m 1st in Grant Co. 7 Jan 1842 Curtis Beauchamp (dec 2 July 1866); m 2nd B. McDonald (dec ca 1874); f mbr Friends; mbr Methodist Ch.; d in Tipton ca 4 June 1889 (8/15/89)

McFEELEY, Alfred - is Grant Co. Sheriff (11/7/89)

McGARVEY, __ - age 5 yr; s M/M Harry McGarvey; d 21 Nov 1899 (11/23/99)

McHENRY, Margaret 'Maggie' - a dressmaker with shop in residence of J.B. Smithson (4/14/92)

McHENRY, T.J. - m; son-in-law of J.B. Smithson; 26 Dec 1895 d at his home in Colorado (1/17/96)

McHENRY, William James - age 5y, 10m, 10da; s Thomas J. and Margaret McHenry; d 11 Aug 1889, bur BC Friends Cem (8/15/89)

McKAIG, Rev. J.W. - Jonesboro M.E. Ch. pastor (4/18/89)

McKEEVER, Charles - f of Jonesboro; recently killed by a train in ND; bur in Jonesboro Cem (7/15/98)

McMASTER, Lawrence - Rau Glass Factory employee (1/11/00)

McMASTER, Nettie - 1892-93 tchr, Little Ridge Sch (8/25/92); - see Nettie (McMaster) BRILES

McNEIL, Loman - a barber in Riley Jay's Barbershop (7/2/97)

McPHERSON, Walter - m Nora Elsie Reeves last Sunday (1/29/97)

McTURNAN, Clare - Rigdon Sch grad; won 2nd Honors in 1899 Liberty Twp. Schs graduation (6/22/99)

McTURNAN, Lawrence - 1891 grad of Liberty Twp. sch (5/21/91)

McWHARTER, Helen (Bogue) - of New Castle; dt Amos H. Bogue and his 1st wife (2/15/00)

MACON, __ - baby of M/M Arthur Macon; bur BC Friends Cem last wk (2/28/89)

MACON, __ - age 14; dt Court Macon; lived just S of East Branch Sch; att East Branch Sch; d 14 Nov 1899 (11/16/99)

MACY, Anna - see George T. PHILLIPS

MACY, F.H. - mbr Fmt. Sch Board (6/15/99)

MACY, Fred - resigns as Supt., Citizen's Gas Co. (1/4/00)

MAIN, __ - age 1 yr; child of M/M Alfred Main; d 22 Aug 1898 (8/26/98)

MAIN, Charles Leroy - b 11 Aug 1868; m Mary Little of Fmt. 14 Aug 1890; mbr Methodists; d 9 Jun 1897 (6/18/97)

MAIN, Julia - mbr Fmt. Women's Relief Corps (11/14/89)

MAIN, William - f of Fmt., now lives in Anderson (3/8/00)

MALLOW, __ - see Mrs. Charles E. EASTES

MALOTT, Nate - owns/operates the Central Hotel (1/24/89)

MALOY, John - mbr of Fmt. Gun Club (9/21/99)

MANG, __ - see Noah JOHNSON

MANLOVE, Bertha May (Mitchel) - b near Rigdon 8 Feb 1880; dt Charles and Eliza Mitchel; 18 Aug 1897 m Leroy Manlove; d 12 Jan 1899 (1/19/99)

MARINE, Emma Jane (Rich) - b Grant Co. 23 Feb 1867; dt Eri and Elizabeth Rich; m 2 Jan 1889 Alfred Marine; d 4 Feb 1896 (2/21/96)

MARINE, Hazel May - b 25 Jun 1894; dt Alfred and Emma Marine; d 13 Oct 1895 (2/21/96)

MARINE, [Nathan] 'Nate' - age ca 50; of 4 mi. E of Fmt.; d 18 Aug 1889 [on Osage Farm] (8/29/89)

MARION NORMAL COLLEGE - started new term last wk (11/19/91)

MARLEY, Iredel - 16 Mar 1892 m Ida Friend in her parents Fmt. home (3/24/92)

MARLOW, __ - age 18m, 2da; child of Dr./M A.F. Marlow; d 25 Jul 1892 (7/28/92)

MARLOW, A.F., M.D. - grad American Eclectic Coll of Ohio, Cincinnati; came to Fmt. ca 1888, has a medical practice (4/14/92)

MARSH, Arminta J. - see Arminta J. RAY

MARSH, D.W.B. - managed Columbia Hotel several yr ago; d 15 Mar 1899 in Cleveland, OH (3/23/99)

MARSH, J.D. - of Summitville; age 68 yr; lived in Madison Co. 46 yr; d 5 Mar 1891, bur Music Cem (3/12/91)

MART, __ - s Oscar and Lizzie C. Mart recently d (8/4/92)

MART, Elma - 1891 grad of Liberty Twp. Sch (5/21/91)

MART, Ettie - m Sammy Mart; d 6 Feb 1889 near Hackleman (2/10/89)

MART, Grace - dt Oscar Mart (12/29/98)

MART, Joseph J. - age 66; Liberty Twp. farmer; hurt by a boar [male swine] last Sunday (12/21/99); of Hackleman area; hog bite has caused a serious mental problem (7/12/00)

MART, Lizzie C. (Scott) - b 30 Jan 1862; dt Stephen (dec) and Rachel Scott of near Oak Ridge; 2 Sep 1882 m Oscar Mart; mbr Oak Ridge Friends; d 16 Oct 1897 (10/22/97)

MART, Nancy (Powell) - of Radley; dt Harrison and Nancy Powell (5/31/00)

MART, [Sarah (Streeter) - wife of Alhambra J. Mart]; d 10 Sep 1892 and her new-born baby d 13 Sep 1892; lived NW of Fmt.; bur BC Friends Cem (9/15/92)

MARTIN, Jacob M. - CW vet bur BC Friends Cem (5/23/89; 6/5/96)

MARTIN, Rhoda - see William HARROLD

MARTIN, Sarah - see Sarah (Martin) STEVENS

MASON, Anna M. - see Anna M. DICKEY

MASON, Esta A. - b Grant Co. 18 Sept 1875; dt G.R. (dec) and S.A. (dec) Mason; d 29 Jan 1891, bur Marion Cem (2/5/91; 2/19/91)

MASON, Florence (Bogue) - of W of Fmt.; dt Amos H. Bogue and his 1st wife (2/15/00)

MASON, Frank - of Hackleman area; last wk m Flora Bogue, dt Amos Bogue (3/7/89)

MASON, Mrs. Jennie - of Hackleman area is mother of Mrs. Anne Highley of Fmt. (2/12/91)

MATCHETTE, Ethel - 1896 grad of Green Twp. Schs (6/5/96)

MATTHEWS, Town of
DREW HOTEL - will soon open with C.M. Houston of Paulding, OH as propriator (1/25/00)
WINSLOW GLASS CO. - incorporated by stockholders Palmer Winslow, Hannah A. Winslow, and H.P. Henshaw; factory will soon be built (9/15/98)

MENDENHALL, A. - mbr/officer Fmt. IOOF (1/4/00)

MENDENHALL, Abigail C. - see Abigail C. HOBSON

MESKIMEN, Nancy - see Thomas Dean DULING, Sr.

METTANK, W.V. - leaves for KS to help thresh wheat (6/28/00)

METTS, Charles H. - new pastor, Fmt. M.E. Ch. (9/1/92)

MIDDLETON, Captolea Jennie (Bailey) - b Decatur Co. 1877; m Walter Middleton 26 May 1896; mbr Fmt. Baptist Ch.; d 17 Feb 1899 (2/23/99)

MILES, J.A. - owns/operates photography studio (4/14/92; 5/22/96); returned from Cuba where he had accompanied 200 Indiana people who wished to set up a colony; he was one of 60 who gave up and returned home (2/1/00); employed by Hartsook Photo Gallery, Marion (3/15/00); and family will soon move to Cuba; is selling his Fmt. property (6/14/00); and family leave for Cuba 28 Nov 1900 (11/8/00); and family left for Cuba at 1:30 PM 27 Nov 1900 (11/29/00), arrived in Cuba 6 Dec 1900 (12/13/00)

MILL TOWNSHIP SCHOOLS
DISTRICT # 3 (DEER CREEK) - tchr, Miss Elva Haisley (3/19/91)
DISTRICT # 4 (NORTH GROVE) - Homer Biddlecum is a student (2/26/97)

MILLER, Mrs. Adam - 9 Feb 1891 celebrated her 63rd birthday (2/12/91)

MILLER, Charles - owns new candy kitchen in north room of Sutton Blk. (1/4/00)

MILLER, Elwood - mbr of Fmt. Gun Club (9/21/99)

MILLER, Isaiah - of Liberty Twp.; brother of Hezekiah Miller and of Mrs. Maria Jones; d 27 Jul 1892, to be bur in Oak Ridge Cem (7/28/92)

MILLER, Maria - see Maria JONES

MILLER, Mary (Haisley) - dt Ira and Rebecca Haisley (9/10/97)

MILLER, Mattie P. - mbr Fmt. Women's Relief Corps (11/14/89)

MILLER, R. Harry - mbr, Fmt. Gun Club (9/21/99); a winner in the 3rd shoot of season at Fmt. Gun Club (7/12/00)

MILLIKAN, Nancy (Davis) - b NC 21 Oct 1828; m Mahlon Millikan 3 Apr 1850; mbr Friends; d 2 May 1892, bur Park Cem (5/5/92; 5/12/92)

MILLINER, __ - age ca 20; dt of widow Milliner; d 22 Jul 1892 (7/28/92)

MILLNER, Miss Maude - of Leesburg, OH is singer with evangelist Hiatt in a revival in Jonesboro Friends MH (10/29/97)

MILNER, Sarah H. - mbr Fmt. Women's Relief Corps (11/14/89)

MINNIC, Mary E. - see Mary E. WRIGHT

MINNIC, Michael - age 90y, 5m, 17da; of Middletown; d recently (3/7/89)

MIRES, Alex - landowner near Fmt. advertising that he permits no hunting on his property (11/12/97)

MISERVEY, Mary - see Asa L. DRIGGS

MITCHEL, Bertha May - see Bertha May MANLOVE

MITTANK, M. - landholder advertising 'no hunting' on his property (10/13/92)

MOLLIN, N.P. - of Liberty Twp.; granted a CW pension of $17 per month (8/27/91)

MONAHAN, James A. - farmer of near Fmt. f lived in Union Co. (12/27/88); 27 Dec 1890 m Addie Turner (1/1/91)

MONAHAN, Michael Edward - b Union Co. 8 May 1873; s James and Susan Monahan; came to Grant Co. In 1882; grad-FFA; att DePauw Univ and Ind. Univ; taught Lake Sch for 3 yr; Principal, Fmt. HS for 3 yr; d recently (1/26/99; 2/2/99)

MONAHAN, William - landholder advertising 'no hunting' on his property (10/13/92)

MONAHAN, Mrs. William - recently d (5/17/00)

MONROE TOWNSHIP SCHOOLS
DISTRICT #10 - T.D. Barr, tchr (11/14/89)

MONTGOMERY, Fern Maria - b 11 Mar 1890; dt John and Ida Montgomery; d 15 May 1892 (5/26/92)

MONTGOMERY, John - mbr, Fmt. Gun Club (9/21/99); a winner in 3rd shoot of season at Gun Club (7/12/00); winner in recent shoot held by Gun Club (11/1/00)

MONTGOMERY, Maria - b Hudson, OH 11 Oct 1849; Nov 1859 m W. Dennis Montgomery; mbr United Brethren Ch.; d 13 Oct 1889, bur BC Friends Cem (10/10/89; 10/17/89)

MONTGOMERY, William Dennis - 2 Jul 1891 m Sarah Kelsey (7/9/91)

MOON, __ - see Mrs. Ed ELLIOTT

MOON, Allen, M.D. - Fmt. physician & surgeon (4/14/92)

MOON, Mrs. Allen - sister of Mrs. W.B. Kimbrough of Marion (7/11/89)

MOON, Ann - see Ann McCOY

MOON, Anna - see Orla SCOTT

MOON, Annie - see Annie DUNCAN

MOON, Caleb - Fmt. area CW vet of Co. K, 130th Ind. Vol. Inf. att his Unit Reunion in Elwood 6 Aug 1896 (8/7/96)

MOON, Eleanor (Hinshaw) - b Highland Co., OH 25 Feb 1810; m 1st 2 Mar 1826 Jesse Holloway (d 5 Nov 1849); m 2nd 5 Aug 1859 Thomas Moon (d ca 23 Jan 1869); joined Methodist Ch. ca 1838; joined Friends ca 1860; d 11 Aug 1892, bur Howe Cem (8/25/92)

MOON, Hattie V. - of Fmt.; has filed for divorce from Samuel Moon (9/7/99)

MOON, Louisa - see Louisa ELLIS

MOON, Luther - s Dr./M Allen Moon; d, bur BC Friends Cem (7/11/89)

MOON, Oscar - mbr Fmt. Friends boy's SS class (1/11/00)

MOORE, Charles Verling - b Montgomery Co. 17 Apr 1849; s Jacob and Tacy Moore; m Mary Baldwin 2 Sep 1874; att Earlham Coll; studied medicene under Dr. Alpheus Henley in Fmt.; 1878 grad- Medical Univ of Louisville, KY; mbr Friends; d 26 Apr 1897 (4/30/97)

MOORE, David - b Grant Co.; age 63; d 20 Jul 1900 at his home in Jonesboro (7/26/00)

MOORE, Frank - 1891 grad of Liberty Twp. sch (5/21/91)

MOORE, Mary W. - mbr Fmt. WCTU (8/8/89)

MOORE, Samuel - age 72; is Jonesboro attorney; wife d ca 1893 (8/26/98); d 15 Jul 1899 (7/20/99)

MOORE, T.M. - of 2 mi. N of Fmt. sells Black Langshan eggs (4/12/00)

MOORE, Willis - f of Fmt.; shot William Swartz in the back in Swayzee a wk ago; Swartz did not die (7/2/97)

MOORE, Willis B.F. - owns Fmt. Brick Works with C.D. Overman (11/26/91; 4/14/92)

MORELAND, __ - baby of M/M Ad Moreland; d 22 June 1889 (6/20/89)

MORELAND, Martha A. - see Martha A. SMITH

MORFORD, George - Fmt. boy who can do bird calls (11/12/91)

MORGAN, Clara - mbr Fmt. Women's Relief Corps (11/14/89)

MORRIS, Arthur J. - 19 Jul 1899 m May Rich, dt M/M Eri Rich (7/20/99)

MORRIS, Luther - unsuccessfully tries to start saloon in Fmt. (5/12/92); has applied for a license to sell liquor in saloon he intends to set up at corner of Main St. & 8th St. (8/18/92); mbr, Fmt. Gun Club (9/21/99)

MORRIS, Micah - Oak Ridge Friends pastor (1/26/99)

MORRISON, William Moses - grad Fmt. HS 1910 (5/10/00)

MOTT, Mrs. Anna - sister of J.B. Smithson (6/3/98)

MOYNIHAN, Daniel - has a cigar and tobacco shop in Fmt. (4/14/92)

MURRAY, __ - see Mrs. D.A. HOLLIDAY

MURRAY, Miss Ida - of Henry Co.; sister of Dr. Holiday's wife (12/29/98)

MYERS, __ - see Mrs. Charles DAUGHERTY

MYERS, Clara - age ca 59; wife of T.D. Myers of Fmt.; d 26 Dec 1897, bur Columbus Grove, OH (12/31/97)

NEAL, __ - see Mrs. J.B. SMITHSON; also
- see Mrs. Alvin WILSON; also
- see Mrs. Micajah WILSON

NEAL, Eli - owns farm 2 mi. S of Fmt. leased by Kelsay Brothers to extract underlying stone (12/17/91); age 69; d 21 Jun 1899 (6/22/99)

NEAL, Mary - see Joseph RICH

NEAL, W.J. - mbr BC W.M. Ch. (4/16/97)

NELSON, Allie - mbr Fmt. WCTU (8/8/89); mbr Fmt. M.E. Ch. (11/5/91)

NELSON, Horace - employed in Wilson's Corner Grocery (7/25/89)

NELSON, Myrtle 'Mertie' - age 8y, 7m, 12da; dt Merriman H. and Allie Nelson; d 26 July 1889 (8/1/89)

NESBIT, John S. - s Cyrus Nesbit; m 28 Jul 1889 Lerena Milholland (8/1/89)

NEWBERGER, Mrs. Jacob - age 78; d at New Cumberland 4 Dec 1899, bur Wabash cem (12/7/99)

NEWBY, Eleazor - mbr BC Friends Cem Improvement Committee (9/1/92)

NEWBY, Exum - purchased SW one-fourth of Section 17 on 28 Dec 1829 (1/7/92)

NEWBY, Marium - see Joseph RICH

NEWBY, Sarah - see Sarah HENLEY

NEWBY, Thomas W. 'Uncle Tommy' - m Sarah 'Aunt Sally' Hill 21 May 1846 in a Quaker ceremony in BC Friends MH; they celebrated their 50th wedding anniv 21 May 1896 at their home 2 mi. S of Jonesboro (5/29/96); in 1893 was a stockholder in Farmers and Merchants Bank (2/22/00)

NEWKIRK, Sarah S. - of Liberty Twp.; is suing husband, William, for divorce; they were m in 1861 (12/17/00)

NEYERS, Sarah (Martin) - see Sarah (Martin) STEVENS

NICHOLSON, __ - child of Ed; d this wk (5/10/00)

NIPP, Vada - see John RINGO

NIXON, Alice - 1896-97 Fmt. Schs 7th grade tchr (3/6/96); 1899-1900 Fmt. Grammer Sch tchr (8/24/99)

NIXON, Inez - dt Alice Nixon (6/14/00)

NIXON, James - mbr BC Friends Cem Improvement Committee (9/1/92)

NIXON, Narcissa - mbr Fmt. Friends Women's Foreign Missionary Society (11/26/91); age ca 82; widow of James Nixon; d 7 Sep 1899 (9/7/99)

NOLDER, Miss Dea - att DePauw Coll (1/7/98); 1899-1900 Fmt. Elementary Sch tchr (8/24/99)

NOLDER, Layton E. - of Fmt.; s Dr. S.M. Nolder (2/4/98); 15 Nov 1898 m Bessie Tigner, dt M/M L.E. Tigner; they will live in Fmt. (11/17/98)

NOLDER, Dr. S.M. - opens medical office in Fmt. (4/2/91); wife is dt James M. and Louisa (Moon) Ellis (7/16/91); b OH; Hahneman Medical Coll of Chicago grad (4/14/92); can now test eyes and supply glasses (8/4/92); is Fmt. physician & surgeon (6/25/97); sold his practice to Dr. W.M. Warner; goes to Newton, KS to practice with his brother (1/14/98); his brother in Newton, KS recently committed suicide (2/4/98); in St. Louis, MO 6 Feb 1898 m Dr. Olive Wilson, f of Fmt. (3/11/98)

NOLIN, Earl - b Johnson Co. 19 Jan 1881; d Fmt. 9 Jul 1900 (7/12/00)

NORRIS, D. - and Bert Pyles arrested for disturbance at Bethel M.P. Ch. on Sunday Jul 17th by pilfering lunch baskets during meeting; each fined $12 by Squire Jones and jailed in Marion when unable to pay fines (7/21/92)

NORTON, Alfred F. - of Fmt. area; brother of Major B.V. Norton (1/28/98); is selling 'Our Mother's Mush,' a cereal food made in California, has ordered a RR carload to sell throughout Indiana (3/2/99)

NORTON, B.V., Major - has grocery (4/14/92); b Essex, England 24 Oct 1816; Sep 1850 came to Grant Co.; m Mary A.; d 17 Jan 1898, bur Gas City Cem (1/21/98; 1/28/98)

NORTON, Frank - starts a new store in Fowlerton (7/31/96); s Major B.V. Norton; is now in California (1/28/98)

NORTON, Jessie - see Jessie FOWLER

NORTON, Marguarete - dt M/M Fred Norton (1/19/99)

NORTON, Mollie - see Mollie COWGILL

NOSE, [Ella] - see William E. GOSSETT

NOSE, Ethel - age 10; d in Liberty Twp. 25 Feb 1891 (2/26/91)

NOSE, Mrs. John - of Fmt.; sister of Joseph Douglas (dec) of Jonesboro (3/9/99)

NOSE, Margaret Jane - see Margaret Jane HINKLE

OAKLEY, Bernice - of Fmt.; age ca 16 (2/8/00)

OAKLEY, Ezra N. - sells clothing in Oakley's Emporium (5/23/89); b Guilford Co., NC 22 Jan 1846; s John (dec ca 1864) and Charity (dec ca 1859); 1st m 1868 to Nancy Thomas (dec ca 1876); m 2nd Sarah J. Hollingsworth ca 1880; d 9 Mar 1897 (3/12/97)

OAKLEY, Fred D. - employee, Oakley's Emporium (7/25/89); is Danville Coll student (9/5/89); will be a clerk in White House Dept. Store (10/1/91); owns a grocery store in Fmt. (4/14/92); s Ezra N. and Nancy (Thomas) Oakley (3/12/97); is Big Four stationmaster (1/19/99)

OAKLEY, Mrs. Fred D. - of Alexandria is dt M/M C.D. Overman of Fmt. (1/17/96)

OAKLEY, Sallie - Secretary, Fmt. WCTU (9/15/98)

OBORN, J.W. - Fmt. M.E. Ch. pastor (1/3/96); is resigning pastorate to return to college (3/13/96)

O'BRIEN, Margaret A. - see Margaret A. COLEMAN

OLDACRE, Sarah E. - see George J. HENSHAW

OLIVER, Henderson - f of Jonesboro; d 19 Feb 1900 in Uniondale, bur Jonesboro cem (2/22/00)

160th INDIANA INFANTRY REGIMENT - Fmt. area mbrs include Corp. Allen Parker, Edgar Baldwin, Will Bishop, Ol Chasey, Burl Cox, Frank DeShon, Hollis Haworth, Charles Payne, Roy Smith, Merton Woollen (1/12/99); David Tappan is mbr Co. A (1/19/99); 2nd Battalion, 160th Ind. left camp at Columbus, GA 15 Jan 1899, boarded transport 'Saratoga' at Charleston, SC; arrived 19 Jan 1899 at Matanzas, Cuba and set up camp 1.5 mi. W of Matanzas (2/2/99); Pvt. George Stout and Corp. George Clothier, both of Co. A, are home on leave (2/23/99); Allen Parker has been discharged; all of 160th Regmt. will be mustered out 25 Apr 1899 (4/6/99)

O'RILEY, Barney - last wk was 1st prisoner in new Fmt. jail (3/9/99)

OSBORN, Miss Flora - b near Fmt. 28 Dec 1871; mbr Fmt. Baptist Ch.; d 20 Jan 1899, bur Harmony Cem, Matthews (1/26/99)

OSBORN, Handley - farmer living 2 mi. SE of Fmt. (11/16/99); skipped town owing money (10/25/00); owns farm 2 mi. S of Fmt.; has returned to wife and family; was in SD; didn't tell wife because he did not want to discuss his trip before he went (11/15/00)

OSBORN, Leona S. - see Clinton JAY

OSBORN, William - prominent early settler in Fmt. Twp. (1/7/92)

OSBORN, Z[imri] C. - landholder advertising 'no hunting' on his property (10/13/92); mbr Pleasant Grove Ch. (4/16/97)

OVERMAN, __ - see Mrs. Fred D. OAKLEY

OVERMAN, Mr. __ - of Marion; tchr, Bethel Sch (12/5/89)

OVERMAN, Clark D. - has a dry goods store (5/16/89); sch tchr ca 1870 (10/17/89); owns, with Willis B.F. Moore, Fmt. Brick Works (4/14/92); owns Overman Brick Yard (10/15/97)

OVERMAN, Edna - will grad 9 Jun 1899 from Fmt. Twp. Schs (6/1/99)

OVERMAN, Edward - m Margaret Lindley 25 Dec 1899 (12/28/99); has a bicycle repair shop on 1st St. (5/3/00)

OVERMAN, J.C. - and wife celebrated 15th wedding anniv. 26 Aug 1898 (9/2/98)

OVERMAN, Linnie - dt M/M C.D. Overman (7/4/89)

OVERMAN, Perna - see Fred DAVIS

OVERMAN, R.E. - teachs music and sells pianos, organs and other musical instruments (4/14/92); organized singing class at Bethel (9/1/92)

OVERMAN, Rebecca - see Rebecca HAISLEY

OXLEY, Rev. __ - pastor of Fmt. United Brethren Ch. (9/13/00)

PADDOCK, W.W. - sells his interest in Fmt. Bowling Alley to E.E. Briles (12/21/99)

PANSY POST OFFICE - established 1 Jul 1892 1.5 mi. S of Center, Liberty Twp. with Jason Biddlecome as Postmaster (7/14/92)

PARK CEMETERY - Park Cem Association is formed; 12 acres were purchased from the Seth Winslow estate; burial plots are laid out prior to sale (4/11/89); Nathan Cox, caretaker (8/27/91); CW vets bur here include: Milton Crowell, Zack Little, John Lillibridge, Z.M. Jones, John Busing, William Powell, Asbury W. Ray, Enoch Beals, Henry McCoy, Benjamin Brewer and Washington Haley (6/5/96)

PARKER, Allen - volunteered for army service during Spanish-American War (4/29/98); Corp. In 160th Ind. Regmt. in Columbus, GA camp (1/12/99); discharged from 160th Ind. Regmt., to take exam for 2nd Lieut. in regular army; s J.H. Parker (4/6/99); passed exam for a commission; enrolled in FFA 24 Apr 1899, will att until ordered to camp (4/27/99); left 17 May 1899 for duty with 25th Regmt. (Colored), may go to Manila, Philippines (P.I.); would have grad from FFA this spring (5/18/99); is stationed at Fort Wingate, NM (6/15/99); of Co. E, 25th Inf., ordered to P.I. (6/22/99); is serving in P.I. (9/21/99); is in trenches 3 mi. N of Manila; is armed with a Colts .38 caliber revolver (9/28/99); is 50 mi. N of Manila (12/21/99); Provost Marshall of Tarlac, P.I. (1/25/00); is in Subig, P.I.; has been under fire 5 times (4/5/00); his mother d 11 May 1900 (5/17/00); is in command of scouts in his area (5/24/00); in command of Co. E, 25th Inf.; may be ordered to China from Manila (8/30/00)

PARKER, B.F. - mbr/officer Fmt. IOOF (1/4/00)

PARKER, Charles T. - employed in Small's Hardware/Implement Store (7/25/89); tchr, Fmt. Twp. Dist. # 2 Sch (12/5/89); is a Fmt. attorney (4/14/92; 7/9/97); mbr Fmt. M.E. Ch. (4/16/97); mbr of Fmt. Gun Club (9/21/99); a winner in the 3rd shoot of season at Fmt. Gun Club (7/12/00)

PARKER, Eliza J. (Rush) - b NC 8 Sep 1846; dt Duncan and Martha Rush; 3 Nov 1872 in Fmt. m Joseph H. Parker; came to IN in 1866; mbr Friends; d 11 May 1900 (5/17/00)

PARKER, Hugh M. - mbr of Fmt. Gun Club (9/21/99); s Joseph H. and Eliza J. (Rush) (dec) (5/17/00)

PARKER, Joseph H. - Pres., Dillon Glass Works (4/14/92); owns/operates Parker's Opera House (8/27/97); mbr of Fmt. Gun Club (9/21/99); m Eliza J. Rush (dec) 3 Nov 1872 (5/17/00)

PARKER, Mark - of Fmt.; s Joseph H. and Eliza J. (Rush) (dec) (5/17/00); a winner in the 3rd shoot of season at Fmt. Gun Club (7/12/00); a winner in recent Fmt. Gun Club shoot (9/20/00; 11/1/00)

PARKER, Robert - of Liberty Twp.; d 19 Jan 1899 of burns when he fell into a hog scalding kettle, bur Park Cem (1/26/99)

PARKS, Lee - has wife and several children; was found wandering around in a dazed condition 3 mi. S of Jonesboro; enroute home from [James] Kirkpatrick farm [Osage Farm], his horse slipped and threw him against a hay baler; Dr. McKinney found that he suffered a brain concussion; d 10 Nov 1898 (11/17/98)

PARRILL, J.W. - of Fmt.; s Mrs. Simons (dec) of E of Fmt. (3/30/99)

PARRILL, Lucy - Fmt. Public Schs tchr (4/2/97; 8/24/99)

PARSONS, H.F. - employed in Hipes' Meat Market; is a Democrat (7/25/89)

PARSONS, Solomon - prominent early Fmt. Twp. settler (1/7/92)

PATENAUDE, Joe - a barber; has bought out Will E. Rudicel's Barber Shop; will operate it (9/14/99)

PATTERSON, Dixie - mbr Fmt. Women's Relief Corps (11/14/89)

PATTERSON, Ella - dt M/M Joseph Patterson; d 27 Dec 1900, bur Park Cem (12/31/00)

PATTERSON, Dr. Joseph W. - att Ind. Medical Coll, Indianapolis (12/27/88); to be awarded MD degree 1 Mar 1889 (2/28/89); 23 Sept 1890 Dr. Lomax signed his Grant Co. Medical Society membership certificate (2/5/91); s Dr. Philip Patterson (4/14/92); purchases brick house on E. Washington St. f owned by Levi Scott (3/11/98); construction starts on his office bldg. on east corner of his new residence property (3/18/98); his new residence is being painted and wallpapered by D.E. Allred (4/22/98); moves his family and his [aunt], Mrs. Libby Baldwin, into his new residence (6/3/98)

PATTERSON, Minnie - dt Dr./M J.W. Patterson; given party 21 Nov 1898 for her 13th birthday (11/24/98)

PATTERSON, Morelan (Pickard) - b 13 Mar 1863; dt Alexander (dec) and Mary Pickard; m 13 Sep 1883 Dr. Joseph W. Patterson; mbr Fmt. M.E. Ch.; d 28 Apr 1896 (5/1/96)

PATTERSON, Dr. Philip - 25 June 1852 Dr. Lomax signed his Grant Co. Medical Society membership certificate (2/5/91); first practicing physcian in Fmt. (4/14/92)

PATTERSON, Owen - of Liberty Twp.; m; arrested for digging ditch under C.I.&E. RR tracks where they cross his farm (10/6/98)

PAUL, J.C. - murdered by Tom Uttley during the Fmt. riot (2/12/91)

PAYNE, __ - see Mrs. Charles WRIGHT

PAYNE, __ - b this wk; dt M/M Zim Payne (10/24/89)

PAYNE, Al. - m; brother of Capt. Dave Payne (dec); d 15 Jan 1898 (1/21/98)

PAYNE, Arl - of Terre Haute; s Thomas Payne (dec) (12/10/00)

PAYNE, Bailey S. - lives at Fmt.; serv Co. K, 130th Regmt. Ind. Vol. Inf. during CW (9/15/92); att his Unit Reunion in Elwood 6 Aug 1896 (8/7/96)

PAYNE, Bessie - sues Blanchard Payne for divorce; they were m in Feb 1889 (5/18/99)

PAYNE, Charles - is in 160th Ind. Regmt. in camp at Columbus, GA (1/12/99); discharged from 160th Regmt., he re-enlisted in a regular army Regmt. (8/31/99); is headed for Philippines (P.I.) (9/21/99); is ill at Jefferson Barracks (10/19/99); is in Honolulu on way to P.I. (12/21/99); is Corp., US Army scouts in the P.I. (6/7/00)

PAYNE, Charles T. - has plumbing shop (4/14/92); is a plumber and gas fitter (1/10/96); celebrated his 31st birthday 30 Apr 1899 (5/4/99)

PAYNE, David - dec in West prior to now (1/15/91)

PAYNE, E.L. - lives at Fmt.; serv Co. K, 130th Regmt. Ind. Vol. Inf. during CW (9/15/92); att his Unit Reunion in Elwood 6 Aug 1896 (8/7/96)

PAYNE, Elsberry - accidentally shot himself in the shoulder recently (6/4/91)

PAYNE, Miss Emma - dt Al Payne (dec); d 8 Oct 1899, bur Bethel Cem (10/12/99)

PAYNE, Hannah Jane 'Jennie' (Cox) - b 5 Nov 1867; dt Nathan and Malinda Cox; 11 Jul 1891 m Mack Payne; d recently (10/13/98)

PAYNE, Capt. James 'Jim' J. - is home from Oklahoma (6/20/89); and wife are camping with another couple for a wk near Mississinewa River (7/18/89); is at Shawnee, Indian Territory (4/24/96); returned home this wk from I.T. where he dug up a buried Indian to get burial property including body 'war paint' (5/22/96)

113

PAYNE, John - of 2.5 mi. SE of Fmt.; age ca 55; m; d 26 Feb 1899 (3/2/99)

PAYNE, John L. 'Dick' - 10 Dec 1900 m Dot Lowney of Alexandria; will live in Fmt. (12/17/00)

PAYNE, Leslie H. - b 21 Mar 1892; s William and Emma Payne; mbr Union Chapel, Fmt. Mission; d 20 Jan 1899 (1/26/99)

PAYNE, Oak 'Shorty' - Fmt. boy; has gone to Oklahoma (7/3/96)

PAYNE, Ralph - Fmt. soldier serving in Philippines (9/21/99); is promoted to Corp. in Philippines (7/12/00)

PAYNE, T.J. - of Fmt. is father of Mrs. Thomas Smith of Charleston, IL (11/17/98)

PAYNE, Thomas - of Fmt.; visits grave of his brother, John M. Payne, in U.S. National Cem, St. Louis, MO (11/5/91); father of Arl and of Mrs. Charles Wright; recently dec (12/10/00)

PAYNE, Zim - 1 May 1889 m Artie Frost (5/9/89); employed in Overman's General Merchandise Store (7/25/89)

PAYTON, John W. - recently was granted a license to retail liquor in Fmt. (10/5/99)

PEACOCK, __ - b 24 Mar 1897; s M/M John H. Peacock (3/26/97)

PEACOCK, Arthur - of Oak Ridge; s Joseph and Cynthia (11/30/99)

PEACOCK, Carlton - of Fmt.; s Joseph and Cynthia (11/30/99)

PEACOCK, Clara Lois - age 2yr, 10m; dt Willis D. (dec) and Cynthia (Fries) Peacock; moves to Charlottesville with mother (11/30/99)

PEACOCK, Cynthia - see Cynthia SMITH

PEACOCK, Cynthia (Fries) - m 16 Jun 1892 Willis D. Peacock (dec); is moving back to Charlottesville (11/30/99)

PEACOCK, Donald - age 6 yr; s Willis D. (dec) and Cynthia (Fries); is moving to Charlottesville with mother (11/30/99)

PEACOCK, 'Lizzie' [Elizabeth S.] - mbr Fmt. Friends Women's Foreign Missionary Society (11/26/91)

PEACOCK, Willis D. - was farmer living near FFA; b New London 18 Jan 1865; s Joseph (dec ca 1867) and Cynthia (now wife of Ephraim Smith of Fmt.); 16 Jun 1892 m Cynthia Fries of Charlottesville; ex-FFA; d 21 Nov 1899 (11/23/99; 11/30/99)

PEARSON, Mrs. 'Angie' [Angelina] - mbr Fmt. Friends Women's Foreign Missionary Society (11/26/91); 17 Feb 1900 is given party for her 55th birthday (3/1/00)

PEARSON, Ella - named as 1896-97 Fmt. Schs 1st grade tchr (3/6/96)

PEARSON, Glen - s M/M Henry Pearson; was given a party 21 Nov 1898 for his 13th birthday in the home of Dr./M J.W. Patterson (11/24/98)

PEARSON, Lemuel - employes 25 men making slack barrel staves (4/14/92); is Fmt. Twp. Assessor candidate (1/25/00)

PEARSON, Mary Eva - see Mary Eva WINSLOW

PEARSON, [Rilla Bell] - see [Rilla Bell] SEALE

PEARSON, W.R. - b Miami Co., OH; and A.W. Ray sell real estate (4/14/92)

PEELE, George W. - tchr at Arcana (1/3/89)

PELL, Rev. Millard - new pastor, Fmt. M.E. Ch. (5/4/99); 1 Aug 1900 m Anna Vandervort of Masontown, WV (9/13/00)

PEMBERTON, Cyrus W. - of Fmt.; joins 29th Inf. Regmt. of regular army; hopes to go to the Philippines (8/24/99); is serving in P.I. (9/21/99); is in Manila (1/4/00); Co. F, 29th US V.I.; arrived Manila 1 Nov 1899; his 1st battle was 19 Dec 1899 (US General

Lawton was killed in that battle); is now at Corregidor (6/21/00); may have been killed or captured recently by Filipinos (10/4/00)

PEMBERTON, Elihu - recently appointed Jonesboro Postmaster (4/18/89)

PEMBERTON, Gladys - age 14m, 13da; dt Loren W. and Leota Pemberton of near Jonesboro; d 13 Jan 1889 (1/17/89)

PEMBERTON, Jesse K. - has farm produce store (4/14/92); mbr BC Friends Cem Improvement Committee (9/1/92)

PEMBERTON, Lem P. - bagged 13 rabbits last Monday (1/7/92); and N.G. Fort own 'The Oak' Barber Shop (4/14/92); recently sold his barber shop to Riley Jay (7/2/97); Charter Mbr, Fmt. Gun Club (6/26/96); one of the winners at a recent shoot sponsored by Fmt. Gun Club at Fmt. Fair Grounds (10/22/97)

PEMBERTON, Mrs. L. - of Jonesboro d 5 Jun 1889 (6/6/89)

PERMAR, Orval Edward - b Fmt. 21 Mar 1897; s William and Winnie [(Monahan)] Permar; d 31 Dec 1899 (1/11/00)

PETERS, Miss Asenath - tchr in colored sch (12/5/89)

PETTIFORD, Edmond - b NC 8 Aug 1795; m 1st Sally Carter (dec ca 1867); m 2nd __ (dec ca 1883); mbr W.M. Ch.; d 30 Aug 1889 (9/5/89)

PETTIFORD, Young - of near Weaver; age 70; d 26 May 1900, bur Weaver Cem (5/31/00)

PETTIJOHN, Naomi - see Naomi GOSSETT

PETTY, __ - see Mrs. Milton COX

PETTY, Charles - of Jonesboro; s Robert P. and Rachel C. (Vestal) Petty (5/17/00)

PETTY, Rachel C. (Vestal) - b Chatham Co., NC 30 Aug 1832; m 6 Oct 1852 Robert Petty; mbr M.E. Ch.; d 8 Jan 1898 (1/21/98)

PETTY, Robert P. - b NC 18 Feb 1836; m Rachel C. Vestal 6 Oct 1853 in IN; d this wk, bur Park Cem beside his wife (5/17/00)

PHILLIPS, George - of North Grove area; is CW vet, does not receive a pension (6/11/91)

PHILLIPS, George T. - 4 Feb 1900 m Anna Macy (2/8/00)

PHILLIPS, Leo H. - b 8 Jan 1892; s John and Mary Phillips (1/14/92); d 13 Apr 1892 (4/21/92)

PICKARD, Alexander - CW vet bur in BC Friends Cem (6/5/96); d ca 1885 (8/24/99)

PICKARD, Bowman - his new blacksmith shop in Fmt. is completed (3/26/91)

PICKARD, John H. - works in a Marion carriage shop (6/6/89); s Alexander (dec) and Mary Pickard (5/1/96)

PICKARD, Mrs. John H. - her parents live in Knox, Starke Co. (9/12/89)

PICKARD, Joseph - s Alexander (dec) and Mary Pickard (5/1/96)

PICKARD, Mary - mbr Fmt. Women's Relief Corps (11/14/89); and dt Alice have new millinary business in north room of Long Bldg. (4/16/91); b Carthage 4 May 1835; 1851 m Alexander Pickard (d ca 1885); mbr Fmt. U.B. Ch.; d 10 Aug 1899 (8/17/99; 8/24/99)

PICKARD, Morelan - see Morelan PATTERSON

PICKARD, Otto - m Audie Leach 21 May 1899 (5/25/99)

PICKARD, W.D. - owns Fmt. blacksmith shop (4/14/92)

PIERCE, __ - age 6 yr; s John Pierce; d 14 Nov 1900 (11/15/00)

PIERCE, Mrs. Sarah - age ca 73; mother of Mrs. Flora A. Bullinger of Fmt.; d in Marion 2 Jan 1892 (1/7/92)

PILKENTON, Annie Frances (Brown) - dt Robert Ray and Mary (Trueblood) Brown (4/27/99)

PITTS, Eunice C. - see Eunice C. HODSON

PODUE, W.M. - and G.A. Brush own an electical supply house (4/14/92)

POLLARD, Lawrence Victor - b 16 May 1891; s Rev./M S.W. Pollard (5/21/91); d 13 Aug 1892, bur in a Grand Rapids, MI cem (8/18/92)

POLLARD, Rev. S.W. - Fmt. Congregational Ch. pastor (1/1/91)

POOL, Joseph - guardian for Rinehardt and Bessie Busing (4/17/96); landowner near Fmt. advertising that he permits no hunting (11/12/97)

POOL, Mattie - see Charles WILSON

POWELL, Cenia V. - b 6 Sep 1887; dt John and Vina L. Powell of Jonesboro; d 26 Apr 1892, bur BC Friends Cem (5/5/92)

POWELL, Elizabeth A. (Humphreys) - mbr Fmt. Women's Relief Corps (11/14/89); b Birmingham Co., KY 26 Dec 1821; dt John and Hannah Humphreys; m William Powell in 1851; mbr W.M. Ch.; d 4 Dec 1897, bur Park Cem (12/10/97;12/24/97)

POWELL, Jonathan 'Johnty' - b Grant Co. 23 Feb 1851; s Harrison and Nancy; never could walk; never m; lived with, sister Mrs. Nancy Mart of Radley; mbr Linwood Friends; d 23 May 1900, bur BC Friends Cem (5/24/00; 5/31/00)

POWELL, Nancy - see Nancy MART

POWELL, William - CW vet bur BC Friends Cem (5/23/89; 6/5/96)

PRESNALL, Alfred M. - is employed in Dale Hardware store (3/18/98); mbr/officer Fmt. IOOF (1/4/00); came to Fmt. ca 1890; d 30 Dec 1900 (12/31/00)

PRESNALL, Frank M. - will teach in a Huntington Co. sch this winter (9/10/91); will teach near Swayzee this winter (9/24/91)

PRESNALL, Mrs. Harvey F. - dt Mrs. E.A. Linn of Stonewall, KY (4/15/98); b Scott Co., KY 19 Jan 1861; m Harvey F. on 8 Mar 1882; mbr Fmt. Friends; has one dt; d 4 June 1898, bur Park Cem (6/10/98)

PRESSNALL, J.F. - pastor of Fmt. W.M. Ch. (1/22/97)

PRETLOW, Dr. Clotilde - physician and surgeon; has office/lives in residence of Mrs. Isaiah Jay on E. Washington St. (12/3/97); now has office in Bank Block (1/14/98)

PUCKETT, Joel - his store at New Corner recently burned (9/5/89)

PYLE, Earl - 1896 grad of Green Twp. Schs (6/5/96)

PYLE, Sarah - see Madison Matthew HAYNES

PYLES, Bert - and D. Norris arrested for disturbance at Bethel M.P. Ch. on Sunday Jul 17th by pilfering lunch baskets during meeting; each fined $12 by Squire Jones and jailed in Marion when unable to pay fines (7/21/92)

RABER, Ed J. - owns/operates Raber Furniture Store (7/25/89); with Ackerman has Raber & Ackerman Furniture Store/Undertaking Parlor (4/14/92)

RADCLIFFE/RATCLIFFE, Rev. J.F. - Fmt. M.E. Ch. pastor (3/12/91; 9/10/91)

RADLEY - named for Samuel Radley who owned land where town is built; name was changed from 'El Morro' because in order to obtain a post office the name could not be compound (1/26/99); Hugh Demick is a local blacksmith (1/18/00)

RADLEY, Samuel - owned land where town of Radley was established on the C.I.&E. RR (1/26/99)

RAILROADS (RR) AND INTERURBAN LINES
BIG FOUR - F.D. Oakley is station master in Fmt. (1/19/99); 3 northbound and 3 southbound passenger trains stop in Fmt. each day (3/15/00)

CHICAGO, INDIANA & EASTERN (C.I.&E.) - a new town on this RR in Liberty Twp. may be named El Morro (9/15/98); Liberty Twp. farmer Owen Patterson is arrested for digging a ditch under RR tracks where they cross his farm (10/6/98); passes through Wright's Station, 2 mi. SW of Fmt. where A.K. Wright & Co. have a large tile factory (10/26/99); RR completed to Converse, is 35 mi. long, all within Grant Co. (11/2/99); has fine passenger station and freight office in Matthews (11/16/99); will carry mail from Fmt. to Leach (3/8/00); a spur track is being laid on Factory Ave. in Fmt. E of and parallel to Big Four tracks; several Factory Ave. residents are opposed to spur line (3/15/00); spur line is completed S of Washington St. (3/29/00); Fowlerton is on this RR (8/1/00); is now completed to Stockport, 6 mi. N of Muncie (11/1/00)
C.W. & M. RAILROAD - completed through Fmt. in summer of 1874 (1/7/92)
CLODFELTER ELECTRIC LINE - Mr. Hayworth, contractor, has 20 teams grading roadbed; have graded from Marion to 2 mi. S of Soldier's Home Bridge, will grade through Jonesboro to Fmt., then through Alexandria to Anderson (6/26/96); work will begin on RR from Fmt. to Marion 3 May 1897 (4/30/97); work on RR continues between Summitville and Anderson and near Gas City (6/18/97); Mr. Cochran is contractor on segment N of Summitville where crews are now working (6/25/97); to go through Jonesboro on Ninth St. (6/25/97); has purchased 37,000 ties (4/1/98); ties are being laid and poles are being set between Jonesboro and Fmt. (4/29/98)
INDIANA TRACTION COMPANY - purchased the Clodfelter Line property (11/26/97); owns Jonesboro-Fmt. gravel pike, has notified its toll gate keepers to stop taking tolls since the pike is in very bad condition (12/31/97)
UNION TRACTION COMPANY - Charles L. Henry is mgr. (8/23/00); is putting in 65' poles to carry electric power (8/23/00); Philip Matter is President (10/25/00)

RAPER, Mrs. [Margaret] 'Maggie' E. - of Middletown is dt Nixon Rush, Sr. (4/2/91)

RATLIFF, Ancil - of Little Ridge is s Joseph Ratliff of Fmt. (12/27/88); tchr, Little Ridge Sch (12/5/89)

RATLIFF, Cornelius - farmer on Deer Creek; killed by a horse in spring of 1882 (10/17/89)

RATLIFF, Joseph - Fmt. Twp. Trustee (4/20/99)

RATLIFF, Milo - att Earlham Coll (6/20/89); tchr for Fmt. Twp. Dist. # 6 Sch (12/5/89); is Earlham Coll student (9/10/91)

RATLIFF, Ryland - b on Deer Creek 1858; s Cornelius Ratliff; started sch 1867 with tchr Asa T. Baldwin; other early tchrs he studied under were Isaac Elliott, C.D. Overman and, at Mississinewa Graded Sch, William Russell; att Spiceland Acad fall 1880-81; began teaching 1881-82 in Van Buren Twp Sch # 3; grad Spiceland Acad 1883; att Marion Normal, then fall 1883 m Emma VanVactor; Center Twp. Sch tchr 1883-84; moved to Fmt. and taught in Fmt. Sch under Elwood O. Ellis 1884-85; went to New Orleans Exposition and to Mammoth Cave in spring 1885; was Fmt. Schs Principal in 1885, then was on faculty of FFA; wife and dt accompanied him summer of 1886 while he att Summer Sch of Science on Martha's Vineyard; they toured New York City, Boston and Washington, DC; fall 1886 took a short course in science at Purdue Univ; returned to faculty of FFA where he remains; mbr Friends; is Clerk, Northern Quarterly Meeting of Friends (10/17/89); mbr Fmt. Friends (4/16/97); Ind. Univ student (9/21/99); in 1893 was a stockholder in Farmers and Merchants Bank (2/22/00)

RATLIFF, Susan - in 1893 was a stockholder in Farmers and Merchants Bank (2/22/00)

RATLIFF, Dr. William N. - of Fmt.; grad-Chicago Dental Coll; buys Fmt. Dental Practice of Dr. N.S. Cox (3/11/98); 27 Aug 1898 m Stella Shugart, dt Henry Shugart of West Branch (9/2/98); dental office is in corner room over Bank (3/8/00)

RAU, Charles - employee, Fmt. Glass Works (9/3/91)

RAU, Fred - employee, Fmt. Glass Works (9/3/91)

RAU, John - and W.C. Winslow own/operate Fmt. Glass Works (4/14/92); recently purchased Fmt. Glass Works for $17,035 (8/12/98)

RAU, Mrs. P.C. - dt Mrs. Robert James of Louisville (1/19/99)

RAY, __ - s of A.W. Ray; is injured by bursting of a gun he was firing (1/3/96)

RAY, Arminta J. - of Fmt.; dt J.D. Marsh (dec) of Summitville (3/12/91); widow of Asbury W. Ray (5/1/96)

RAY, Asbury W. - is Fmt. Justice-of-the-Peace (4/25/89); serv CW in 79th Ind. Inf. (9/24/91); b Fmt. Twp. 27 Jul 1842; and W.R. Pearson sell real estate (4/14/92); b Grant Co. 27 Jul 1842; s Charles and Sarah Ray; m Jane Marsh 18 Jul 1867; serv US army 3 yr during CW; mbr Friends; d 23 Apr 1896 (5/1/96); bur in Park Cem (6/5/96)

RAY, Bob - hunted rabbits with Millard Clark and Gib LaRue last Fri. (12/5/89)

RAY, James - has volunteered for army service during Spanish-American War (4/29/98)

REASONER, __ - b 5 Feb 1897; s M/M George Reasoner (2/5/97)

REASONER, George - and family move to LaGlora, Cuba (10/25/00); to go to Cuba 28 Nov 1900 (11/8/00); and family left for Cuba at 1:30 PM 27 Nov 1900 (11/29/00), arrived in Cuba 6 Dec 1900 (12/13/00)

REASONER, H.D. - in 1893 was a stockholder in Farmers and Merchants Bank (2/22/00)

REECE, Charity - see Jesse WRIGHT

REECE, Emma J. - see Emma J. HOFFMAN

REED, A.L. - mgr., Big Four Window Glass Factory (8/30/00)

REED, Phoebe - see Phoebe HUSHAW

REEVES, Nora Elsie - see Walter McPHERSON

RELFE, Frank - s Warren Relfe; age 17; recently enlisted in army (9/7/99)

RELFE, Walter - left for KS last wk to help thresh wheat (6/28/00)

REYNOLDS, Edith - mbr Oak Ridge WCTU (6/3/98)

RHODES, Harvey O. - of Mill Twp. m Rachel in 1871; charging desertion, files for a divorce (11/14/89)

RHODES, John - age 16; s Harvey O. and Rachel Rhodes (11/14/89)

RHODES, Ollie - age 9; s Harvey O. and Rachel Rhodes (11/14/89)

RHODES, Osman - age 12; s Harvey O. and Rachel Rhodes (11/14/89)

RIBBLE, Hort - Fmt. soldier serving in P.I. (9/21/99); of Co. H, 34th US Inf.; is in Honolulu enroute to Manila (10/12/99); in camp at Presidio, CA after escorting prisoners from P.I. (12/24/00)

RICE, Sarah (Martin) - see Sarah (Martin) STEVENS

RICH, ___ - b 26 Sep 1897; dt M/M Alson W. Rich of Hackleman area (10/1/97)

RICH, Emma Jane - see Emma Jane MARINE

RICH, Joseph - b Randolph Co., NC 6 May 1811; s Peter and Sarah; 13 Jun 1836 m Marium Newby in Hamilton Co.; 21 Sep 1863 in Grant Co. m 2nd Mary Neal (dec 1881); 18 May 1882 m 3rd Malinda Cox (dec 1886); 14 Sep 1886 m 4th Margaret Draper (dec 14 Dec 1895); mbr Friends; d 3 Jul 1896 (7/10/96)

RICH, May - see Arthur J. MORRIS

RICHARDSON, Hopkins - prominent early settler in Fmt. Twp. (1/7/92)

RICH, Elias - divorced his wife several yr ago in Liberty Twp. where she still lives; Elias and s Stranton moved to Kansas ca 1884; recently they were charged with hog stealing and on 16 Apr 1889 Elias was captured and Stranton was shot dead near Topeka, KS (4/18/89)

RICH, Nettie (Jones) - dt M/M H.A. Jones; in her father's home m Elwood Rich 8 Oct 1892 (10/13/92)

RICH, Rebecca - sister of Jesse H. Rich; d 30 Apr 1896, funeral at BC Friends MH (5/1/96)

RICH, Rosa - see Perry SEALE

RICHARDS, Eva - dt M/M J.H. Richards of near Matthews; lived in Fmt. until 1893; d 22 Apr 1899 (4/27/99)

RICHARDS, J.H. - came to Fmt. ca 1888; now sells real estate and insurance (4/14/92)

RICHARDS, Rena - see J.W. HIMELICK

RICHARDSON, Mrs. Charity - of Liberty Twp. d 6 Aug 1892 (8/11/92)

RICHARDSON, Zimri - of Jonesboro; d 27 May 1900 (5/31/00)

RIDDLE, Frank - employee of Big Four Glass Works (5/22/96)

RIDDLE, Will - age 16; s Frank Riddle; injured CW vet when he threw a piece of iron through the window into a railroad coach; is arrested (5/22/96)

RIGDON, Bazel T. - age ca 86; d 30 May 1898 (6/3/98)

RIGDON, Dr. Pryor - of Rigdon (town was named for him); age 85; d 28 Oct 1900 (11/1/00)

RILEY, Rev. C.A. - Fmt. Congregational Ch. pastor (10/1/97); and family have gone to Moline, MI where he will pastor a Congregational Ch. (2/1/00)

RILEY, David J. - his residence was used 26 Feb 1889 for Catholic services (2/28/89); f of MI; lived in Fmt.; d 25 Sep 1898 (9/29/98)

RILEY, Rev. G.P. - of Marion; in a 'Wesleyan Herald' article Riley is accused by W.H. Kennedy, acting in behalf of the Indiana Conference of the W.M. Ch., of: (1) speaking evil of the 'holiness doctrine,' and (2) lying; these charges are signed by Jacob Hester and W.J. Seekins, W.M. Ministers; Riley published a letter defending himself, stating that 2 works of grace are not necessary for salvation and that the holiness doctrine has only been espoused for 3 yr by a splinter group of W.M. (8/29/89); Editor, 'Child's Golden Voice;' Scott's Opera House used by Riley's supporters for a 7:30 PM meeting, 500 people attended; Riley disproved accusation that he had left the W.M. Ch., he also justified his stand against the 'extravagancies of the holiness faction for their absurd claims and practices;' meetings of the Indiana Conference of W.M. refuse to allow him to speak in his own defense (9/5/89); is Associate Editor of the 'Wesleyan Herald;' was refused membership in Mich. Conference, W.M. Ch. because 'he is member of Indiana Conference' (9/12/89); has affidavits signed by Congregational Ch. officials attesting that he did not join that body as was charged by the Indiana Conference of the W.M. (11/14/89); of Marion; enlisted in an Ohio regmt. early in CW, was Colonel of a colored regmt.; was preacher for over 40 yr; while pastoring Fmt. W.M. Ch., he joined GAR; Wesleyans expelled him from the ministry because they believed the GAR to be a 'secret organization;' now mbr of M.E. Ch. (12/31/91); 'Father Riley' lives in Marion; has 'Boys Brigade' of over 50 boys set up to keep boys from learning evil/bad associations on the streets (6/19/96)

RINGO, Carrie A. - see Benjamin F. KIMES

RINGO, John - of Oak Ridge; 24 Dec 1898 m Vada Nipp of Roseburg (12/29/98)

RITTENHOUSE, H. - mbr/officer Fmt. IOOF (1/4/00)

RITTENHOUSE, Miss Ollie - Oak Ridge Sch grad; won 1st Honors at 1899 Liberty Twp. Schs graduation (6/22/99)

ROADS - a gravel road is being made E from Little Ridge to toll gate S of Fmt. on the Fmt.-Summitville Pike (9/1/92)

ROBERTS, __ - child of Joseph Roberts of near Fmt.; d 22 Feb 1891 (2/26/91)

ROBERTS, Brooks - leaves for KS to help thresh wheat (6/28/00)

ROBERTS, J.W. - has a harness shop in Fmt. (4/14/92)

ROBERTS, Miss Pearl - severely burned last Sunday while cooking at Keely's Boarding House in Fmt. (10/26/99); d of burns 6 Nov 1899 (11/9/99)

ROBERTS, Tessie - age 16; dt Joseph Roberts; d 5 Apr 1899 (4/13/99)

ROBINSON, Ed - Big Four Glass Factory employee (1/18/00)

ROBINSON, M.D. - a winner in the 3rd shoot of season at Fmt. Gun Club (7/12/00)

ROBISON, Laura - see John W. DAVIS

ROLL, Vall - Charter Mbr of Fmt. Gun Club (6/26/96)

RONEY, Elias M. - of Fmt.; recently awarded a military pension (2/5/91); 18 Feb 1897 and wife celebrated their 50th wedding anniv (2/26/97)

ROOSE, Cyrus - from Cincinnati, OH; purchases Central Hotel from A.B. Loutzenhiser (10/22/91)

ROOSEVELT, Theodore - came to Fmt. by rail at 8:50, spoke to 4,000 people for 10 minutes asking them to re-elect President McKinley (10/11/00)

ROSE, Sarah E. - see Asa L. DRIGGS

ROUSH, Mrs. Fremont - of near Jonesboro is dt M/M Robert Hasting (3/6/96)

ROUSH, Mrs. Mary - of E of Gas City; age 84; m Isaac Roush (dec Sep 1896) 27 Mar 1834; has 11 children, all living; d of burns 4 Apr 1897 (4/9/97)

ROUSH, William P. - of Gas City area; CW vet of Co. H, 12th Ind. Regmt.; att party with other Co. H mbrs 6 Jan 1899 (1/12/99)

RUDICIL, Will E. - has a Shaving Parlor in Fmt. (4/16/97); sold out to Joe Patenaude who will operate it (9/14/99)

RUDICIL, Mrs. Will E. - dt Mrs. Lafe Griffith of Sheridan (10/26/99)

RULEY, Mahala - age 86; widow of R.W. Ruley, f Grant Co. Treas.; d 2 Aug 1900 (8/9/00)

RUNK, __ - see Ananias FRAZIER

RUSH, __ - infant dt of Walter and Mary Rush; bur BC Friends Cem 15 Jul 1891 (7/16/91)

RUSH, Alfred - s Duncan and Martha (5/17/00)

RUSH, Calvin C., Jr. - att Earlham Coll (9/24/97; 1/7/98); 1898-99 Lake Sch tchr (2/2/99); is Earlham Coll student; will grad in Jun (12/28/99; 5/17/00)

RUSH, Eliza J. - see Eliza J. PARKER

RUSH, Mrs. Elwood - 12 Jul 1896 is given dinner for her 61st birthday (7/17/96)

RUSH, Helen D. - see Milton A. GIBSON

RUSH, Rev. Henry - of KS; s Duncan and Martha (5/17/00)

RUSH, Iredell - prominent early settler in Fmt. Twp. (1/7/92)

RUSH, John B. - f of Fmt. Twp.; d 11 May 1891 in Wabash (5/14/91)

RUSH, Joseph - CW vet bur BC Friends Cem (5/23/89; 6/5/96)

RUSH, Miss Louie - Liberty Twp. Sch # 12 tchr (4/4/89); - see E. GARNER

RUSH, Louisa - Fmt. WCTU mbr (2/7/96)

RUSH, Margaret - see Margaret WILLIAM(S)

RUSH, [Margaret] 'Maggie' E. - Mrs. Maggie E. RAPER

RUSH, Mary (Wilson) - sister of Daniel Wilson of Wabash; d 26 Jul 1891 (7/30/91)

RUSH, Millicent - see Elwood HAISLEY

RUSH, Nixon, Sr. - b Randolph Co., NC 13 Jan 1814; s Azel and Elizabeth; m 1832 Demaris Burnes; d 25 Mar 1891, bur BC Friends Cem beside his wife (3/26/91; 4/9/91)

RUSH, Olive - takes position as illustrator for 'Harper's Weekly' (11/1/00)

RUSH, Walter - returns from Cuba where he had accompanied 200 Indiana people who wished to set up a colony; he was one of 60 who gave up and returned home (2/1/00)

RUSH, Walter C. - has truck farm near FFA; is in a confused state of religious ferver recently; confessed that he set off the explosion that wrecked the Morris Saloon in Fmt. on 15 Aug 1893; he claims that Thomas Nixon and Alexander Henley were with him at the time; he also claims that he returned and set fire to the bldg. the next night; no one supports his statements (9/3/97)

RUSSELL, William - tchr, Mississinewa Graded Sch ca 1875 (10/17/89)

ST. JOHN, __ - see Mrs. James BROWN

SANDERS, Bernice - 30 Oct 1899 given party for her 15th birthday (11/2/99)

SANDERS, Geneva - 1896-97 Fmt. Schs 6th grade tchr (3/6/96; 4/2/97); 1899-1900 Fmt. Grammer Sch tchr (8/24/99); - see Walter L. JAY

SCHMUCK, Rev. Eli - preached at Center Christian Ch. last Saturday and Sunday nights (1/22/91)

SCHOOLEY, Rachel J. - see Rachel J. McDONALD

SCOTT, __ - young dt of Leander Scott of Oak Ridge; d 25 Dec 1898 (12/29/98)

SCOTT, Alvin - 29 Jun 1889 m Emma Luther (7/4/89)

SCOTT, Annis (Arnett) - b NC 9 Feb 1819; dt Jesse and Margaret Arnett; m 20 Apr 1836 James Scott; mbr Friends; d 29 Jan 1892 (2/11/92)

SCOTT, Eli - m; s Stephen Scott (dec) (11/7/89)

SCOTT, Elmina - see Elmina BOGUE

SCOTT, Rev. Elwood - m; s Stephen Scott (dec) (11/7/89); Carthage Friends pastor; performed marriage of his brother, Levi to Emilie R. Hill (11/19/91); of Carthage is s Rachel Scott of Fmt. (2/16/99)

SCOTT, Emilie R. (Hill) - dt of Mrs. Nancy H. Hill of Carthage; m Levi Scott 10 Nov 1891 (11/12/91)

SCOTT, Emiley - mbr Fmt. Women's Relief Corps (11/14/89)

SCOTT, H.A. - is new prop., Columbia Hotel; is installing a bathtub in hotel (2/16/99)

SCOTT, James - of Fmt.; 29 Jan 1891 m Mary E. Browning of Bloomfield, OH (2/5/91)

SCOTT, James - not m; brother of Stephen Scott (dec) (11/7/89); 26 Dec 1990 given party for his 76th birthday (1/1/91); is 84 yr old (11/3/98)

SCOTT, Jesse - Supt., Fmt. Canning Co. (3/24/92)

SCOTT, Levi - Trustee, Fmt. Congregational Ch. (2/10/89); Cashier, Farmers' and Merchants' Bank (7/25/89); m; s Stephen Scott (dec) (11/7/89; 11/12/91); mbr Fmt. Congregational Ch. bldg. committee (12/19/89); is elected to FFA Board of Trustees (12/25/89); 10 Nov 1891 will m Emilie R. Hill of Carthage (11/5/91); and wife are on railroad tour to Washington, D.C. and the east (11/12/91); an owner of Fmt. Canning Co. and of Hoosier Packing Co. in Xenia (3/24/92); owns Scott's Opera House; Sec./

Treas., Dillon Glass Works (4/14/92); and family have moved from Laporte, TX to Burlington, IA (11/12/97)

SCOTT, Lindley - m; s Stephen Scott (dec) (11/7/89); owns a clothing store with __ Davisson (4/14/92)

SCOTT, Lizzie C. - see Lizzie C. MART

SCOTT, Minta (Hollingsworth) - m 1st __ Lottridge; lived in Fmt.; 7 Oct 1900 m E.J. Scott, Alexandria grocer (10/11/00)

SCOTT, O.R. - Fmt. insurance, loan, and real estate man since 1888 (4/14/92)

SCOTT, Oliver - 1891 grad of a Liberty Twp. sch (5/21/91); 17 Mar 1898 m Anna Baker (3/25/98)

SCOTT, Orla - 9 Sept 1889 m Anna Moon (9/12/89)

SCOTT, Stephen - b Wayne Co. 21 Jul 1821; came to Liberty Twp in 1849 with wife Mahala (dec 1856); m 2nd Rachel Cloud in 1858; brother of James Scott of Fmt.; mbr Friends; d 1 Nov 1889 (11/7/89)

SCOTT, Stephen - pastor, Little Ridge Friends (9/2/98)

SCOTT, Mrs. Stephen - Little Ridge WCTU vice president (6/3/98)

SCOTT, Tom - of near Matthews; had 27 sheep killed and several more hurt by dogs Monday night (7/2/97)

SCOTT, William - m; s Stephen Scott (dec) (11/7/89)

SEALE, Allen - dec; s William P. and Elizabeth W. (Henley) Seale (12/5/89)

SEALE, Alvin - att Danville Normal Coll (6/25/91); leaves for Stanford Univ where he will be a student (7/7/92); is riding a bicycle west to Stanford Univ; on Jul 12th rode across Mississippi River at St. Louis (7/21/92); still on way to Stanford Univ, he is in a hunting camp 45 mi. W of Colorado Springs; will be there 2 more wk; has walked to the top of Pike's Peak twice (9/1/92); Stanford

Univ student; went with Hopkins-Knowles Arctic Expedition to study birds/fish in northern Alaska recently (8/27/97); is near Dyea, Alaska working for Geology Dept. of Cambridge Museum, notes the greed and poor clothing of the gold seekers (3/11/98); Asst. Curator, Dept. of Ornithology, Calif. Academy of Science (6/15/99); stationed in Honolulu, Hawaii (5/3/00); described a new petrel collected on Kauai by Francis Gray; is collecting birds on Guam for the Bishop Museum of Honolulu (9/20/00)

SEALE, Arthur E. - 28 Sep 1898 m Ella Kennedy, dt M/M William Kennedy of Fmt.; will live in Denver, CO (9/29/98); and wife live in Denver, CO (10/25/00)

SEALE, Bertha - att Earlham Coll (12/6/00)

SEALE, E.J. - Liberty Twp. Trustee candidate (1/18/00)

SEALE, Edmond H. - b near Fmt. 27 Nov 1861; s William P. and Elizabeth W. (Henley) Seale; m Lottie B. Hiner 27 Apr 1884 at Harvard, IL; mbr Friends; d 2 Jul 1891, bur Park Cem (7/9/91); his widow, Lottie, m a Mr. Freer, moved to Howard, IL; d last wk (2/26/97)

SEALE, Elizabeth W. (Henley) - b Grant Co. 11 Aug 1839; dt Phineas and Mary (Bogue) Henley; m 20 June 1860 William P. Seale; mbr Fmt. Friends; lived W of Fmt.; d 14 Nov 1889, bur BC Friends Cem (11/21/89; 12/5/89)

SEALE, Ella - dec dt William P. and Elizabeth W. (Henley) Seale (12/5/89)

SEALE, Dr. I.N. - resigns as Liberty Twp. Trustee (9/22/98); and wife live in Hackleman (7/19/00)

SEALE, John Bert - att DePauw Univ; s William P. and Elizabeth W. (Henley) Seale (11/21/89; 12/5/89); m Elva Haisley of Oak Ridge 14 Oct 1891; will live on his farm 1.5 mi. W of Fmt.; is a wealthy Friends minister (10/15/91); mbr of Fmt. Friends bldg. committee (2/11/92); a gas well is being drilled on his farm (8/1/00)

SEALE, J.P. - is Univ of Michigan student (6/19/96)

SEALE, John, Sr. - leaves for England; will be gone all winter (10/27/92)

SEALE, Johny - of Hackleman; has new 'cork' leg (7/12/00)

SEALE, Mrs. Johny - of Hackleman; sister of Emma (Cox) Cammack (6/28/00)

SEALE, [Martin] Luther - brother of Arthur E. Seale of Denver, CO (9/22/98)

SEALE, Pearl- Univ of Michigan student (10/8/97); senior, Univ of Michigan Medical Sch (9/29/98)

SEALE, Perry - 24 Dec 1890 m Rosa Rich, dt M/M Jesse Rich of N of Fmt. (12/25/90)

SEALE, [Rilla Bell] (Pearson) - b Hendricks Co. 1875; dt M/M Henry Pearson; m [Martin Luther] Seale; d 17 Sep 1898, bur Park Cem (9/22/98)

SEALE, William P. - b England; s Elijah J. and Elizabeth Seale of Plaiston, Essex Co., England; m Elizabeth W. Henley 20 June 1860; lives W of Fmt. (12/5/89); returned home from visit in England with wife he married while there (11/5/91)

SEEKINS, Rev. W.J. - signed list of charges against Rev. G.P. Riley (8/29/89); is W.M. pastor of Sheridan, IN (9/5/89)

SEELEY, Fred - a winner in shoot at Fmt. Gun Club (7/12/00)

SEELY, Mrs. Sarah - of Hackleman area; sister of Jerry Hartly; d recently (5/21/91)

SELBY, John - landholder advertising 'no hunting' on his property (10/13/92)

SHANE, Mrs. Joseph - d last wk, bur Park Cem (7/19/00)

SHARP, James - is a glass blower in Fmt. Glass Works (11/12/91)

SHEEDY, James - tchr, Rigdon Sch (12/5/89)

SHELTON, Julia A. - see Gabriel 'Gabe' JOHNSON

SHERWIN, Bert - a barber in Riley Jay's Barbershop (7/2/97)

SHERWIN, Frank - tchr, East Branch Sch (1/1/91); resigns as East Branch tchr (1/8/91); East Branch tchr this fall (9/3/91)

SHERWIN, William Howl - b OH during CW; father d in CW; 1879 moved with his mother to Pt. Isabel; att Rigdon Sch; att Ladoga Normal Sch; tchr 1 yr in Rigdon Sch; att summer sch at Ind. Univ; tchr 1 yr at Oak Ridge Sch; now he and his brother, Frank, are selling merchandise in Pt. Isabel (10/31/89); b Westboro, OH July 1864; att Ind. Univ. in 1887; taught in Oak Ridge Sch; d recently (1/1/91)

SHIDELER, Ezra - leaves KS to help thresh wheat (6/28/00)

SHIELDS, Al - landowner near Fmt. advertising that he permits no hunting on his property (11/12/97)

SHUEY, A.W. - and J.M. Bloomer own/operate a Fmt. restaurant/ boarding house purchased from __ Galloway (4/14/92); has sold his restaurant (10/13/92)

SHUEY, Allen - mbr Fmt. Congregational Ch. (4/16/97)

SHUEY, Mrs. Ethel - will be a performer in the 'Holiday Musicale' sponsored by the Fmt. IOOF Lodge and given in Parker's Opera House on 30 Dec 1897 (12/24/97)

SHUGART, Rev. Con - will hold a Memorial Day service at White Egg (5/21/91)

SHUGART, Henry - lives in West Branch area (9/2/98)

SHUGART, Isaiah - age 54; of Liberty Twp. d 21 Jun 1892, bur Odd Fellow's Cem (6/23/92)

SHUGART, Ras - of Deer Creek area; age 30+; s John Shugart; m; d 27 Apr 1892 (5/5/92)

SHUGART, Stella - see William N. RATLIFF

SHULL, Alonzo - 1896 grad, Green Twp. Schs (6/5/96)

SHULTZ, Fred - left for KS last wk to help thresh wheat (6/28/00)

SHUT, David - left for KS last wk to help thresh wheat (6/28/00)

SIBERLING, Monroe - of Kokomo; is arranging for the construction of his brick home in Jonesboro at cost of $50,000 (6/18/97)

SIEGEL, Ed - 1 Nov 1891 m Clara Dillon (11/5/91)

SILVERS, Albert - age ca 23; s Myers Silvers of Herbst; while att the Grand Opening of William Comer's new general store in Coles [Station] 21 Apr 1900, being of a quarrelsome disposition and drunk, shot Al Glessner in the forehead; now Glessner has signed a complaint against Silvers (4/26/00)

SIMONS, Mrs. __ - of E of Fmt.; d recently (3/30/99)

SIMONS, Carl - of Matthews; s Adriel Simons; FFA student; d 10 Oct 1900 (10/18/00)

SIMONS, Henry - landholder advertising 'no hunting' on his property (10/13/92)

SIMONS, John - 31 Mar 1891 m Ruth Stalker (4/2/91)

SIMONS, Levi P. - mbr of Salem Ch. (9/10/91; 4/16/97)

SIMONS, Mrs. Matthew W. - d 11 Feb 1891; will be bur Windfall (2/12/91)

SIMONS, P.T. - left for KS this wk to help thresh wheat (6/28/00)

SIMONS, Perry - is Purdue Univ student (9/28/99)

SIMONS, W.D. - left for KS last wk to help thresh wheat (6/28/00)

SIMONS, Wilson - 11 Mar 1891 m Mattie Corn, both are of Leachburg area (3/19/91)

SISSONS, E.P. - owner/operator, Fair Store (7/25/89)

SISSONS, Mary E. - mbr Fmt. Women's Relief Corps (11/14/89)

SLATER, Margaret 'Maggie' - 29 Jan 1900 was given party for her 16th birthday (2/8/00); lives near Matthews; att FFA (5/3/00)

SLUDER, I.N. - and F.M. Wood own Wood & Sluder Saw Mill; employs 30 to 50 men (4/14/92)

SMALL, __ - see Mrs. Charles WILTSIE

SMALL, Albert - is Earlham Coll student (12/29/98)

SMALL, Cornelius R. - sells hardware and farm equipment in his store across street from Fmt. Post Office (4/25/89); has largest hardware store in this part of Indiana (7/25/89); Supt., Fmt. Friends SS (7/9/91); Fmt. Friends bldg. committee mbr (2/11/92); sells life insurance (6/7/00)

SMALL, Effie - dt M/M C.R. Small; FFA student (1/4/00); att Earlham Coll (12/6/00)

SMALL, Elvira J. - mbr Fmt. Friends Women's Foreign Missionary Society (11/26/91)

SMALL, Enoch - over 30 yr ago in Jonesboro blew the first steam whistle ever heard in Grant Co. (1/29/97)

SMALL, Noah - b Grant Co. 21 Feb 1839; f of Fmt. and of Marion; was a miller at Union Mills, IN in 1866; m; d in Anderson 6 Mar 1899, bur Matlock Cem, Wabash Co. (3/9/99)

SMALL, Oliver - of Amboy is FFA student (1/7/98)

SMILEY, James A. - b 19 Aug 1887; s Noah and Amanda Smiley; d 1 May 1899, bur Park Cem (5/4/99; 5/11/99)

SMILEY, Joseph W. - in 1893 was a stockholder in Farmers and Merchants Bank (2/22/00)

SMITH, __ - see Mrs. John A. HUNT

SMITH, __ - infant of M/M Roland Smith d 10 Jun 1889 (6/13/89)

SMITH, __ - baby of M/M Fred Smith d 30 Apr 1899 (5/4/99)

SMITH, Al - contracted to do carpentry on new Little Ridge Sch (3/24/92)

SMITH, Ansel - of Marion is s Ephraim Smith of Fmt. (5/24/00)

SMITH, B. - mbr/officer Fmt. IOOF (1/4/00)

SMITH, C.S. - Fmt. W.M. Ch. pastor (11/29/00)

SMITH, Charles W. - s Thomas W. Smith (11/29/00)

SMITH, Mrs. Charles W. - of Fmt.; dt W.R. Fowler of near Rushville (2/2/99)

SMITH, Clarkson - 1891 grad of a Liberty Twp. sch (5/21/91)

SMITH, Cynthia - m 1st Joseph Peacock (d ca 1867); m 2nd Ephraim Smith of Fmt. (11/30/99)

SMITH, E. - Fmt. Town Clerk (6/25/97); Supt., Fmt. Water Works (10/8/97)

SMITH, Ed - is a shoemaker/cobbler in Fowlerton (3/12/97)

SMITH, Estella - see Estella COX

SMITH, J.B. - Fmt. area CW vet; att a Vet Reunion in Elwood 6 Aug 1896 (8/7/96)

SMITH, Martha A. (Moreland) - b near Jonesboro 25 Feb 1838; dt David and Mary H. Moreland; m William Smith 16 Oct 1858; lived on farm S of Fmt. except for 5 yr in KS; mbr M.E. Ch.; d 15 Jan 1897, bur Park Cem (1/22/97; 2/5/97)

SMITH, Roland - his 35-yr old mare d 19 Apr 1891; first horse he ever owned, given to him by his father (4/23/91)

SMITH, Roy - is in 160th Ind. Regmt. in camp at Columbus, GA (1/12/99)

SMITH, Scytha - Fmt. WCTU member (2/7/96)

SMITH, Miss Thana - ex-FFA; d recently, funeral held in Upland (2/8/00)

SMITH, Thomas W. - age 77; d 27 Nov 1900, bur Park Cem (11/29/00)

SMITH, William H. - officer in Beeson Post, GAR (12/10/91); lives at Fmt.; serv Co. K, 130th Regmt. Ind. Vol. Inf. during CW (9/15/92); att his Unit Reunion in Elwood 6 Aug 1896 (8/7/96); his wife Martha d 15 Jan 1897 (2/5/97)

SMITH, Zula - of Fmt.; 11 Aug 1897 given party for her 17th birthday (8/13/97)

SMITHSON, baby - dt of M/M Jake Smithson d 6 Oct 1892 (10/6/92)

SMITHSON, Adeline - see Adeline WOOLEN

SMITHSON, Cora - 28 Mar 1889 was given party for 15th birthday (4/4/89)

SMITHSON, David 'Dave' E. - is opening a drug store in Caldwell, Idaho (8/18/92); of Emmett, Idaho; s J.B. Smithson of Fmt. (2/11/98)

SMITHSON, Isaac - sells gravestones (9/17/91)

SMITHSON, J.B. - sister is wife of Dr. B.D. Snodgrass of Marion (12/27/88); of Fmt.; CW vet (3/28/89); CW pension increases from $4 to $8 per month (5/14/91); officer, Beeson Post of GAR (12/10/91); and John S. Baker have a contracting & building firm; McHenry Dressmaking Shop is in his residence (4/14/92); att a Vet Reunion in Elwood 6 Aug 1896 (8/7/96); brother of Mrs. Anna Mott and Nancy Snodgrass of Muncie (6/3/98)

SMITHSON, Mrs. J.B. - sister of William Neal of Marion and of Mrs. Micajah Wilson of Fmt. (3/25/98)

SMITHSON, Jonathan - CW vet bur in BC Friends Cem (6/5/96)

SMITHSON, Lydia - mbr Fmt. Women's Relief Corps (11/14/89)

SMITHSON, S. - mbr/officer Fmt. IOOF (1/4/00)

SMITHSON, Susie - mbr Fmt. Women's Relief Corps (11/14/89)

SNODGRASS, Rev. __ - Jan 1890 will become Center Christian Ch. pastor (12/12/89)

SNODGRASS, M.M - prop., Big Four Barbershop; has installed a bath in his shop (3/8/00)

SNODGRASS, Nancy (Smithson) - of Muncie is sister of J.B. Smithson (6/3/98)

SOMMERVILLE, J. - leaves for KS to help thresh wheat (6/28/00)

SPENCE, Will - constructed the new milk wagon owned by A.J. Wilson (9/2/98)

SPURGEON, Joseph Worth - b Adams Co., OH ca 1851; att Marion HS 8 wk in 1868; taught 4 yr in Center Sch and 2 yr in Howell Sch, both schs are in Liberty Twp.; d Oct 1885 (12/26/89)

STALKER, __ - age 15; s William S. Stalker; d 7 Nov 1891, bur BC Friends Cem (11/12/91)

STALKER, Ruth - see John SIMONS

STANFIELD, Hannah Ann - see Jacob Reese WRIGHT

STANFIELD, Lydia Jane - see Lydia Jane BALDWIN

STANLEY, Mrs. A.E. - of San Diego, CA; dt Thomas and Lydia Baldwin (5/25/99)

STANLEY, Jim - without provocation, struck crew foreman David Drook with a rock on the job site where crews are constructing the Clodfelter RR line N of Summitville, Drook was taken to Fmt. and is expected to recover (6/25/97)

STARR, C. Asbury - Fmt. area CW vet of Co. K, 130th Ind. Vol. Inf. att his Unit Reunion in Elwood 6 Aug 1896 (8/7/96); has a fruit stand at Main & Washington St. (6/7/00); has moved his fruit stand from bank corner to Washington & Adams St. (6/14/00)

STARR, John Porter - grad Fmt. HS 1900 (5/10/00)

STARR, Osha - 1896-97 Fmt. Schs 5th grade tchr (3/6/96); has enrolled in DePauw Univ. (4/2/97); 1899-1900 Fmt. Grammer Sch tchr (8/24/99)

STEARNS, Rev. F.B. - of Michigan is new Fmt. Congregational Ch. pastor (1/25/00); has resigned and returned to MI (5/24/00)

STEINHIZER, __ - see Mrs. Van WRIGHT

STEVENS, Sarah (Martin) - b near New London, OH in 1841; dt M/M Jacob N. Martin; m 1st Col. Rice (dec) of Venton, IA; m 2nd A.J. Neyers (dec); m 3rd 21 Nov 1884 B.F. Stevens in Aberdeen, SD; mbr Fmt. Congregational Ch.; d 11 May 1900, bur Marion IOOF Cem (5/17/00)

STEWART, Al[va] - of Hackleman area; d last wk, bur BC Friends Cem (9/24/91)

STEWART, Myrtle - age 7; dt Mrs. Thomas Helm of Michaels; d of burns 22 Sep 1900 (9/27/00)

STIVERS, Jack - Editor/prop., 'Fmt. News' (12/27/88); stable at his home burned in fire of 1 Oct 1892 that destroyed several Fmt. business' (10/6/92)

STONER, Dr. J.J. - of Marion drove his auto through Fmt. last Monday; 1st auto in Fmt. and 1st auto in Grant Co. (11/2/99); has a Sanitarium at Boots St. & 5th St., Marion (3/8/00)

STOREY, Charles - Purdue Univ student (3/19/91)

STOUT, George - Pvt., Co. A, 160th Ind. Regmt. is home on leave (2/23/99)

STREETER, Sarah - see Sarah MART

STUART, __ - see Ivy LUTHER

STUART, Mary - see Mary KEARNS

STUART, Rebecca - b Randolph Co., NC 12 May 1804; m John Stuart (dec); her dt m Ivy Luther; mbr Friends; d 7 Sept 1889, bur BC Friends Cem (9/19/89)

SUGAR, Margie - ca age 16; of Fmt. (2/8/00)

SUGAR GROVE - is 1 mi. W of Jonesboro (6/21/00)

SUGAR GROVE DITCH (Fmt. Twp.) - will soon be constructed; bids for work are being sought (6/25/97)

SULLIVAN, J.A. - mbr of Fmt. Gun Club (9/21/99)

SULLIVAN, Jennie Pearl - see Jennie Pearl KIMES

SUMMITVILLE, Town of
COWGILL TILE FACTORY - operated by Samuel Cowgill (1/25/00)

SUTTON, Mrs. Jennie - 9 Apr 1900 will open millinery shop in Sutton Block, S. Main St. (4/5/00)

SWAFFORD, Chris - of Jonesboro; m __ Green, dt William Green (10 Nov 1898 d at age 111) (11/17/98)

SWAIM, Mrs. Amanda - d 17 Jul 1900 at her home in Noblesville; bur Gas City Cem (7/19/00)

SWAIM, J.L. - and W.H. Wiley own a lumber yard (4/14/92)

SWARTZ, Chris - landholder advertising 'no hunting' on his property (10/13/92)

SWOPE, Frank - sells his blacksmith shop to Elmer Flint (12/27/88)

SYMONS, J.W. - 6 Apr 1889 was given party for 35th birthday (4/11/89); is Fmt. Marshall (5/16/89)

TAPPAN, David - mbr Co. A, 160th Ind. Regmt. (1/19/99)

TATE, Lousina - see Oliver 'Bod' P. WEAVER

TAYLOR, Lydia J. (Leavelle) - age 55; dt Henry Leavelle; mbr W.M. Ch.; d 31 May 1900 (6/7/00)

TAYLOR, Will - s Lydia J. (Leavelle) Taylor (6/7/00)

TEMPLETON, __ - b 15 Jan 1889; dt M/M Charles Templeton (1/17/89)

TEMPLETON, Mrs. J.W. - d 21 Feb 1889 (2/21/89)

THOMAS, __ - baby of M/M Lon Thomas; d 24 July 1889 (7/25/89)

THOMAS, __ - child of M/M Lon Thomas; d last wk (7/28/92)

THOMAS, __ - child of M/M Hanley Thomas; d 7 Aug 1898 (8/12/98)

THOMAS, Chart - employee, Beasley Drug Store (7/25/89)

THOMAS, Eli - [husband of Alice C.]; mbr BC Friends Cem Improvement Committee (9/1/92)

THOMAS, Elijah - of Jonesboro d 20 July 1889 (7/25/89)

THOMAS, Frank - of Fmt.; sues his wife, Maggie for separation (3/1/00)

THOMAS, John - is being held in Marion jail with a deranged mind (7/26/00)

THOMAS, Mary - wife of Dr. W.B. Thomas; d 1 Jan 1888, bur BC Friends Cem (1/3/89; 1/10/89)

THOMAS, Nancy - see Ezra N. OAKLEY

THOMAS, Peter - b SC 24 Jun 1801; came to IN ca 1813; m twice; mbr M.E. Ch.; d 6 Jun 1900, bur BC Friends Cem (6/21/00)

THOMAS, Miss Sadie - age 26; d 21 Jan 1900, bur Park Cem (1/25/00)

THOMAS, Mrs. Snead - of Marion; d recently (10/26/99)

THOMAS, Solomon - prominent early settler in Fmt. Twp. (1/7/92)

THOMAS, Walter R. - of Henry Co.; s Chart Thomas of Fmt. (10/3/89)

THOMAS, William - 14 Feb 1897 m Cora E. Atkinson (2/19/97); lives in Fmt.; is being sued for divorce by wife, Cora (12/31/00)

THORN, Arthur - leaves for KS to help thresh wheat (6/28/00)

THORN, George W. - of Fmt.; CW vet of Co. H, 12th Ind. Regmt.; att party with other Co. H mbrs 6 Jan 1899 (1/12/99)

THRIFT, Charles - age ca 20; FFA student; att Fmt. W.M. SS; d 8 Aug 1889, bur BC Friends Cem (8/15/89; 8/22/89)

THURSTON, George W. - in 1893 was stockholder in Farmers and Merchants State Bank (2/22/00)

TIGNER, Bessie - see Layton E. NOLDER

TIGNER, C.M. - General Manager, Dillon Glass Works (10/15/91; 4/14/92)

TIGNER, Ed - of Fmt.; mgr., King City Glass Works (7/17/96)

TIGNER, Goldie - had party 20 Mar 1899 for her 11th birthday (3/23/99)

TIGNER, Juliette - and Mabel are daughters of Mrs. E.E. Tigner of Matthews (5/25/99)

TINGLEY, Frank - s Marshall F. Tingley; was working in Jamaica for US Weather Bureau; is now ill in Havana, Cuba (9/7/99); is in Fmt. recovering from recent illness (9/28/99)

TOMLINSON, Noah - leaves for KS to help thresh wheat (6/28/00)

TRADER, Doll - s Samuel Trader; d 18 Sep 1899 (9/21/99)

TRADER, Robert - owns farm 2 mi. S of Fmt. leased by Kelsay Brothers to extract underlying stone (12/17/91)

TRADER, Mrs. Robert - of 2 mi. S of Fmt.; age ca 63; m; d 11 Mar 1899, bur Park Cem (3/16/99)

TROTT, Cora - see H. Lewis KEPLER

TROTT, Elcie - b TN; age 63; mother of Mrs. H.L. Kepler; d in Fmt. 8 Jul 1892, bur New Hope Cem, Howard Co. (7/14/92)

TROY, Catherine - see Will LaRUE

TRUEBLOOD, Mary - see Robert Ray BROWN

TRUELOCK, J.T. - of Gas City; during CW serv Co. D, 7th Ind. Cav. (10/12/99)

TURNER, Addie - see James A. MONAHAN

TURNER, George - has a military pension (3/12/91)

TUTTLE, Emaline - see Emaline BALDWIN

TUTTLE, J. - Trustee, Fmt. W.M. Ch. (2/10/89)

TUTTLE, Orilla B. - b Madison Co. 1 Feb 1863; dt James and Hannah Tuttle; d 27 Aug 1889, bur Marion (8/29/89; 9/5/89)

TWEEDY, Marion - purchased Riley Jay's barbershop (10/17/89)

TYLER, J.J. - m; given surprise birthday party 15 Jun 1896 (6/19/96); quit lumber and milling business; and wife move back to North Manchester (2/26/97)

ULRICH, infant - child M/M Andy Ulrich; d 13 Oct 1900 (10/18/00)

UMSCHIED, Constantine - is divorcing his wife, Cora E. (10/1/97)

UNDERWOOD, James - d 2 Jan 1889, bur BC Friends Cem (1/3/89)

UTTLEY, Tom - found guilty of the murder of J.C. Paul during the Fmt. riot; sentenced to 2 yr in the State Penitentiary (2/12/91)

VANDERVORT, Anna - see Rev. Millard PELL

VanVACTOR, Emma - see Ryland RATLIFF

VanWINKLE, William Milton - b Sulphur Springs 22 Aug 1858; 1st taught in Green Twp at age 20; grad Lebanon Coll 1882; taught in Rigdon Sch; after 1882 taught in Center and Howell Schs; admitted to the bar Feb 1884, practiced law before Judge Brownlee; d 18 July 1884, bur Knox Chapel Cem (11/7/89)

VAUGHN, Frank - returns to Fmt. after 3 yr serv in regular army; is discharged (6/22/99); serv in Philippines (9/21/99)

VAUGHN, George W. - a Fmt. gunsmith (4/23/91; 4/14/92); a winner at shoot sponsored by Fmt. Gun Club at Fmt. Fair Grounds (10/22/97); and E.E. Hiatt re-activate Fmt. Gun Club (9/21/99); a winner in 3rd shoot of season at Fmt. Gun Club (7/12/00); a winner in recent Fmt. Gun Club shoot (9/20/00; 11/1/00)

VEISLET, Leopold - age 13 yr; s M/M Leopold Veislet; recently drowned in Mississinewa River at dam below the old bridge at Jonesboro (6/10/98)

VERNON, Francis 'Frank' M. - b 7 Mar 1850; m Lydia Lane 1 Feb 1872; mbr W.M. Ch.; d 12 Feb 1899 (2/16/99)

VESTAL, Rachel C. - see Rachel C. PETTY

VETOR, Mrs. John - 22 May 1889 is given a party for her birthday (5/23/89)

VIGUS, DR. C.B. - Medical Doctor; is a Fmt. Physician & Surgeon (5/22/96); shares office with Dr. A. Henley (3/5/97); now of Summitville; 20 Oct 1897 will m Ione Latham, dt M/M T.P. Latham of Fmt. (9/24/97)

VINSON, __ - baby of M/M Will F. Vinson d 1 Aug 1892 (8/4/92; 8/11/92)

VINSON, Nathan - and wife of Fmt. will celebrate 50th wedding anniv 20 Mar 1899 (3/16/99)

VINSON, Miss Stella - 21 Mar 1897 celebrated her 21st birthday (3/26/97)

WAGGY, Rachel - b near Richmond 12 Sep 1826; m Philip Waggy ca 1851; f mbr Friends; d Upland 21 Aug 1899 (8/24/99)

WALDEN/WALDRON, Alfred - CW vet bur in unmarked grave in BC Friends Cem (5/23/89; 6/5/96)

WALKER, Hattie (Little) - m; dt M/M Alex Little; lives in Peoria, IL (12/1/98)

WALKER, Mrs. Sallie -V. President of Matthews WCTU (11/10/98)

WALKMACK, Addie - b 7 Oct 1890; dt Will and Ella Walkmack; d 28 Apr 1899 (5/4/99)

WALTHALL, D. - gives notice that Robert L. Wilson will have charge of Evergreen Cem in Walthall's absence; apply to Wilson for lots (2/7/89)

WALTHALL, Ezra - of Jonesboro has lots for sale in Evergreen Cem (9/7/99)

WARD, Austin P. - b Grant Co. 9 Jun 1839; m Lucinda A. Easter 29 Jan 1860; joined Pleasant Grove M.P. Ch. 1889; lived in Fmt.; d 28 Sep 1898 (9/29/98; 10/6/98)

WARD, Mrs. William - age 34; d 6 Jun 1889, bur BC Friends Cem (6/13/89); dt of Mrs. Sarah Barden of Rochester (6/20/89)

WARDWELL, W.S. - has charge of Fmt. Woolen Mill (4/18/89)

WARE, Joe - landowner near Fmt. advertising that he permits no hunting on his property (11/12/97)

WARE, William - Leachburg Sch tchr (3/19/91; 9/3/91)

WARNER, Dr. W.M. - purchased the Fmt. practice of Dr. S.M. Nolder (1/14/98)

WEAVER - town post office will be discontinued when Fmt. begins rural free mail delivery (3/22/00)

WEAVER, Miss Amanda - of Marion; will give weekly dancing lessons in the Parker Opera House (9/29/98)

WEAVER, Augustus - Fmt. barber, m 20 Oct 1889 __ Bell of St. Joseph, MI (10/24/89); brother of Oliver 'Bod' Weaver (2/15/00); wife is Lulu (2/22/00)

WEAVER, Oliver 'Bod' P. - Fmt. barber; b 4 Sep 1854; s James I. and Elizabeth; brother of Augustus of Fmt. and of Philander, Levi, and Thomas, all of Carthage; ca 1888 m Lousina Tate; mbr Baptist Ch.; d 15 Feb 1900, bur Park Cem (2/15/00; 2/22/00)

WELLS, Miss <u>Flora</u> - 1891 grad of a Liberty Twp. sch (5/21/91); will teach 1897-98 in Little Ridge Sch (6/25/97);
- see Amos BANNISTER

WELSH, Edward - Bell Window Glass Factory bookkeeper is promoted to office manager (6/28/00)

WELTY, W. - recently bought the Columbia Hotel from J.W. Deaner (11/19/97)

WESCOTT, Mary Louisa - see Mary Louisa GATES

WESTON, Capt. Hugh - CW vet att a Vet Reunion in Elwood 6 Aug 1896 (8/7/96); landowner near Fmt. advertising that he permits no hunting on his property (11/12/97)

WHARTON, Mrs. Alice - president of Matthews WCTU (11/10/98)

WHEELER, H.I. - Charter Mbr, Fmt. Gun Club (6/26/96); one of the winners at a recent shoot sponsored by Fmt. Gun Club at Fmt. Fair Grounds (10/22/97)

WHEELER, Jasper N. - owner, Wheeler's Mill (4/14/92); b [Beardstown], IL 11 Jan 1841; moved to NC with parents until CW; in Hancock Co. [14 Apr 1863] m Mary J. Butler (d ca 1877); m 2nd Sallie Ledbetter ca 1900; mbr Fmt. Odd Fellows Lodge; d 3 Oct 1899 (10/5/99; 10/12/99)

WHISLER, Elias J. - of Jonesboro; d 1 Nov 1892 (11/3/92)

WHITE, Belle - Fmt. WCTU mbr (4/2/97)

WHITE, J.W. - tchr in colored sch (12/5/89)

WHITE, Rev. Levi - new pastor, Fmt. Congregational Ch. (8/7/96); resigns to take a pastorate elsewhere (7/2/97)

WHITE, Riley F. - employee, Oakley's Emporium (7/25/89)

WHITE EGG - Friends soon to build MH here (1/15/91); almost $1,000 has been raised for new MH (1/29/91)

WHITE'S TRAINING SCHOOL AND ORPHAN'S ASYLUM [WHITE'S INSTITUTE, Wabash Co.] - Supt. W.A. Mills resigns and returns to Indianapolis; Lewis Hockett of Fmt. will be new Supt. (4/2/97)

WHITNEY, Harry O. - m Luzena F. Cowgill 2 Jul 1896 (7/10/96); is in Colorado for his health; his wife is going to him (5/24/00)

WHITNEY, L.R. - employee, Farmer's and Merchant's State Bank (10/8/91)

WHITNEY, Roland T. - tchr, Grant Sch (12/5/89); tchr, BC Sch (9/3/91); quit teaching at BC Sch (10/8/91)

WHITSON, James - of Jonesboro; serv CW as a paid substitute of Isaiah R. Shugart (3/17/92)

WHYBREW AND FLANAGAN DITCH - Gilbert LaRue and others have petitioned for its construction starting at BC N of Fmt. and to run E for 4 mi. (2/26/97)

WHYBREW, Daniel - mbr BC Friends Cem Improvement Committee (9/1/92)

WHYBREW, William - landholder advertising 'no hunting' on his property (10/13/92)

WIEDENHOEFT, Rev. William - pastor of Fmt. Congregational Ch. (12/19/89)

WILBERN, Rev. J.M. - preaches at Little Ridge Friends 2nd Sunday of each month (8/15/89)

WILCUTS, Clark - m Anna Brown 23 Nov 1892 in her parents home in Marion (12/1/92)

WILDLIFE - at least 20 persons advertise that they will allow no hunters on their land during this hunting season (10/13/92)
BOBWHITE QUAIL - season is now open (10/17/89); John T. McCombs of Hackleman area recently killed 45 quail with 3 shots (12/25/90); hunting season closes 20 Dec 1891 (12/17/91); quail were scarce during the 1896-97 hunting season (7/16/97); quail season is open Nov 10 - Dec 31 (10/15/97)
FOX - a fox drive may soon be held (2/10/89); there will be a fox drive in Monroe Twp. 19 Dec 1900; schools will be dismissed for it (12/13/00); the Monroe Twp. fox drive failed to get any fox (12/20/00)
MASTODON - bones of mastodon are being unearthed on the Hodson farm near Upland by Prof. Ward of Taylor Univ (8/20/97)
OPOSSUM - mbrs and pastor at Hill's Chapel A.M.E. Ch. at Weaver will have a possum dinner on Christmas Day (12/24/91)
PASSENGER PIGEON - A. Williamson of Sweetser recently killed a wild [passenger] pigeon, presumeably in or near Sweetser (3/30/99)
RABBIT - Millard Clark, Gib LaRue, and Bob Ray shot 14 rabbits in 2.5 hours last Friday (12/5/89); Lem Pemberton bagged 13

WILDLIFE (continued)
rabbits last Monday; 4 other local hunters bagged 36 rabbits same day (1/7/92)
RATTLESNAKE - Hen Gillispie recently killed a black rattlesnake near Lake Galatia (7/2/91)
SQUIRREL - new law makes it illegal to hunt squirrels between Dec 20 and June 1 (4/4/89); season is now open (6/20/89)

WILEY, Harry - a winner in the 3rd shoot of season at Fmt. Gun Club (7/12/00)

WILEY, W.H. - and J.L. Swaim own a lumber yard (4/14/92)

WILKINSON, F.B. - one of the partners starting the new Borrey Window Glass Factory (4/29/98); office mgr., Bell Window Glass Factory, resigns, moves to Logansport (6/28/00)

WILLIAM(S), Margaret (Rush) - of Gas City; dt Duncan and Martha Rush (5/17/00)

WILLIAMS, Marion - of Hackleman; m; d 7 Apr 1900, bur Knox Chapel Cem (4/19/00)

WILLIAMSON, A. - of Sweetser; recently killed a wild [passenger] pigeon (3/30/99)

WILSON, __ - see Mrs. Z.M. GOSSETT

WILSON, Mr. __ - 1899-1900 tchr, Pansy Sch, Liberty Twp. (10/19/99)

WILSON, A.J. - owns new milk wagon constructed by Will Spence (9/2/98)

WILSON, Mrs. Alvin - of Fmt. is dt of William Neal of Marion (3/4/98)

WILSON, Blanche - 23 May 1899 was given party for her 14th birthday (5/25/99)

WILSON, C.M. - s M/M Milton Wilson of Wabash (10/24/89); brother of Daniel Wilson of Wabash (1/25/00)

WILSON, Charles - 11 Sep 1897 m Mattie Pool; will live 3 mi. S of Fmt. (9/17/97)

WILSON, Chester - att Purdue Univ 1899-1900 (6/14/00)

WILSON, Clark - of Fmt.; s Jesse E. And Hannah (Hill) Wilson (4/13/99)

WILSON, Clark - set up his dental office in Jonesboro recently (6/19/96)

WILSON, Cyrus - of Fmt.; s Jesse E. And Hannah (Hill) Wilson (4/13/99)

WILSON, Eunice P. - [of near Fmt.]; is Grant Co. WCTU President (4/3/96); recently assisted in establishing Matthews WCTU (11/10/98)

WILSON, Hannah (Hill) - b NC 6 Mar 1821; dt Aaron and Nancy Hill; came to Grant Co. ca 1828; m 21 Jun 1838 Jesse E. Wilson (dec 1883); mbr Friends; d 11 Apr 1899 (4/13/99)

WILSON, Hattie (Bixbey) - wife of Nate A.; sells hats and bonnets (4/14/92)

WILSON, J.H. - weighs 125 lbs.; owns/operates BeeHive Grocery & Dry Goods (7/25/89); started 'Beehive' ca 1881 (4/14/92); 25 Oct 1899 m Miss Etta Long, dt Mrs. Fred Norton, Sr.; will live in Fmt. (10/26/99)

WILSON, Jep/Jap - lives with his father S.C. Wilson 2 mi. N of Fmt. (6/25/97); is Fmt. Deputy Postmaster (3/30/99)

WILSON, John - s Samuel Wilson (2/26/91)

WILSON, John - of Logansport; s Jesse E. And Hannah (Hill) Wilson (4/13/99)

WILSON, Lin - Fmt. Twp. Trustee candidate (1/18/00)

WILSON, Mrs. Margaret - was given party for her 73rd birthday 1 Nov 1898 (11/3/98)

WILSON, Mary - see Mary RUSH

WILSON, Micajah - brother of Samuel C. Wilson (3/19/91); and wife were m over 50 yr ago (11/3/98)

WILSON, Mrs. Micajah - of Fmt. is sister of William Neal of Marion and of Mrs. J.B. Smithson of Fmt. (3/25/98)

WILSON, Nate A. - Fmt. merchant; 1 Jan 1889 m Hattie Bixbey of Wabash; live in Fmt. (1/3/89; 1/10/89); and wife own/operate Wilson's Corner Grocery (7/25/89)

WILSON, Dr. Olive (Charles) - wife of Clark Wilson; att Women's Medical Coll, Chicago (1/3/89); and son return to Chicago medical sch (10/3/89); grad 30 Mar 1891 M.D. (4/2/91); opens medical office in her residence, Main & 12th St. (5/7/91); President, Grant Co. Women's Suffrage Assn. (9/10/91); recently set-up medical practice in Carrolton, MO (4/24/96); - see Dr. S.M. NOLDER

WILSON, Robert L. - has charge of Evergreen Cem in absence of D. Walthall (2/7/89); mbr BC Friends Cem Improvement Committee (9/1/92)

WILSON, Mrs. S.C. - dt of Thomas Jessup of Rush Co. (4/14/92)

WILSON, Thomas - CW vet bur BC Friends Cem (5/23/89; 6/5/96)

WILSON, Will E. - employed by J.H. Wilson in BeeHive (7/25/89); resigns from Bee Hive Grocery, buys Latham's Vehicle & Harness Manufacturing Co. (4/8/98); mbr of Fmt. Gun Club (9/21/99)

WILSON'S FORD - on Mississinewa River; Sun. 19 May 1889 several persons were baptized here (5/23/89); 5.5 mi. NE of Fmt.; crosses Mississinewa River; 43 persons were baptized here last Sun. (5/22/96); FFA class of 1896 had picnic here 2 Jul 1896 (7/3/96)

WILTSE, __ - b 20 Mar 1889; dt M/M Charles Wiltse (3/28/89)

WILTSIE, Charles A. - and wife celebrated 13th wedding anniv recently (8/7/96)

WILTSIE, Mrs. Charles - dt Noah Small (dec) (3/9/99)

WILTSIE, Florence - Treasurer, Fmt. WCTU (9/15/98)

WILTSIE, Gertrude - dt M/M Charles A. Wiltsie (8/7/96)

WILTSIE, Grace - dt M/M Charles A. Wiltsie (8/7/96)

WIMSETT, Jesse W. - b 27 Jan 1898; s Charles and Mary; d 8 Sep 1900 (9/13/00)

WINKS, FRANK - head miller for Fmt. Mills (2/7/89)

WINSLOW, __ - see Mrs. Jesse BOGUE; also - see Mrs. Lew CASSELL

WINSLOW, __ - age ca 6 months; child of Thamer Winslow; d 16 Feb 1892 (2/18/92)

WINSLOW, __ - young child of M/M Ancil Winslow d 2 Mar 1892 (3/3/92)

WINSLOW, __ - b 9 Aug 1892; s M/M Denny Winslow (8/18/92)

WINSLOW, Addie - mbr Fmt. WCTU (8/8/89); wife of Will C. Winslow (10/24/89)

WINSLOW, Albert - s Henry Winslow; Fmt. soldier serving in Philippines (9/21/99)

WINSLOW, Ancil - came home 24 Dec 1888 after living a yr in Nebraska (12/27/88)

WINSLOW, Mrs. Anna - an original Grant Co. settler, moved to IA ca 1855, is now visiting in Fmt. (10/24/89)

WINSLOW, Mrs. Anna - Little Ridge WCTU treasurer (6/3/98)

WINSLOW, Daniel - b Randolph Co., NC; age 80; came to Jonesboro area in 1829; d 18 May 1889 at Jonesboro, funeral at BC Friends MH, E.O. Ellis was minister-in-charge (5/23/89)

WINSLOW, E.L. - mbr/officer Fmt. IOOF (1/4/00); is a Fmt. sign painter (6/28/00)

WINSLOW, Edith Fair - dt of Will C. and Addie Winslow; d 29 Sept 1889 (9/26/89; 10/3/89; 10/24/89)

WINSLOW, Elizabeth Jane (Little) - b Randolph Co., NC; age ca 56; m Cyrus Winslow 25 Dec 1873; mbr Friends; d 15 Dec 1897 (12/24/97)

WINSLOW, Florence - dt of Will Winslow (9/26/89)

WINSLOW, Hugh Walker - had a 'claim' in Dakota at the beginning of the CW but had to abandon it because of Indian troubles; says 'the noble red man' is in the imagination of novelists, Indians will steal anything (2/28/89); with W.H. Hasting, owns a Fmt. meat market; owns/operates Winslow & Sons Livery Stable; drove stage from Marion to Anderson ca 1860 to ca 1874 (4/14/92); livery stable burns 1 Oct 1892 (10/6/92); and wife celebrated 50th wedding anniv 22 Feb 1898 (2/25/98; 11/3/98); 16 Jan 1900 had 73rd birthday (1/18/00)

WINSLOW, Hannah A. - a stockholder in the Winslow Glass Co. of Matthews (9/15/98)

WINSLOW, Irvin B. - grad Fmt. HS 1900 (5/10/00)

WINSLOW, J.W. - and family moved from Fmt. to southern Dakota ca 4 yr ago and now have returned and live in Marion (10/24/89)

WINSLOW, Jabez N. - s Hugh Walker Winslow (4/14/92)

WINSLOW, Jane (Henley) - dt John and Margaret Henley; m Jonathan P. Winslow 1 Feb 1844 (8/24/99; 4/12/00); mbr BC Friends; d 16 Dec 1890 (12/25/90)

WINSLOW, Jesse - b Randolph Co., NC 16 May 1802; s Henry and Elizabeth; m 1826 Penina Henley; mbr BC Friends; d 16 Dec 1890 (12/25/90)

WINSLOW, John - employed in Fmt. Bank (7/25/89)

WINSLOW, John H. - s Hugh Walker Winslow (4/14/92); narrowly escaped death when office of livery stable where he sleeps burned along with the stable and several business' at 4:20 A.M. 1 Oct 1892 (10/6/92)

WINSLOW, John H. - b NC 20 Feb 1857; s Jonathan P. and Jane H.; never m; att Earlham Coll and Valpraiso Normal; d 28 Oct 1897, funeral in Fmt. Baptist MH (10/29/97; 11/5/97)

WINSLOW, Jonathan Phelps - b Randolph Co., NC 11 Jun 1818; s Hardy and Christina; 1 Feb 1844 m Jane Henley; att New Garden Boarding Sch (now Guilford Coll, NC); taught sch for several terms; moved to Fmt. in 1860; d 18 Aug 1899, bur Park Cem (8/24/99)

WINSLOW, Joseph - prominent early settler; purchased NW one-fourth of Section 17 on 28 Dec 1829 (1/7/92)

WINSLOW, Leslie - s Jabez Winslow (10/11/00)

WINSLOW, Lizzie - see Frank WRIGHT

WINSLOW, Lizzie (Dillon) - see Lizzie DAUSE

WINSLOW, Mabel - studies violin at Metropolitan Sch of Music, Indianapolis (1/12/99)

WINSLOW, Mary - won 2nd place in the WCTU silver medal speaking contest held at Bethel M.P. Ch. last Sunday (9/3/97)

WINSLOW, Mary Eva (Pearson) - age 25y, 8m; dt Henry C. and Minerva Pearson; m Denny Winslow; d 1 Sep 1892 (9/8/92)

WINSLOW, Mary L. (Jean) - lived E of Fmt.; b Guilford Co., NC 3 Sep 1857; dt Phillip and Mary A. Jean; 7 Oct 1880 m Webster J. Winslow; d 2 Jun 1892 (6/9/92)

WINSLOW, Matthew - Dec 1829 purchased W 1/2 of NE 1/4 of Sec. 17 (1/7/92)

WINSLOW, Micajah - see Lizzie DAUSE

WINSLOW, Nancy Alice - b near Jonesboro 24 Feb 1856; dt Levi and Mary E. Winslow; d Marion 23 Nov 1891 (12/3/91)

WINSLOW, Nettie Maude (Johnson) - dt Gabriel and Julia A. (Shelton) Johnson; m Jabez Winslow (6/21/00)

WINSLOW, Nixon - Fmt. Friends bldg. committee mbr (2/11/92); is President of Citizen's Exchange Bank (3/20/96)

WINSLOW, Ora - mbr East Branch Friends (4/16/97); President, Fmt. WCTU (9/15/98)

WINSLOW, Palmer - a stockholder in Winslow Glass Co. of Matthews (9/15/98); and wife are moving to Fmt. from Matthews (6/28/00)

WINSLOW, Seth - 28 Dec 1829 purchased W 1/2 of NE 1/4 of Sec. 20 (1/7/92)

WINSLOW, Seth B. - oldest s of H. Walker Winslow; m; living in Greensburg, working as a freight engineer for Big Four RR when killed 30 Jul 1897 in a train wreck (7/30/97)

WINSLOW, Thomas - of E of Fmt.; f sch tchr; is Republican candidate for Grant Co. Surveyor (1/3/96); is Grant County Assessor candidate (2/1/00)

WINSLOW, Mrs. Thomas - 18 Aug 1892 was given surprise party for her 34th birthday (8/25/92)

WINSLOW, Webster J. - m Mary L. Jean 7 Oct 1880; lives just E of Fmt. (6/9/92)

WINSLOW, Wick - s Cyrus and Elizabeth J. (Little) Winslow (12/24/97); lives in Swayzee (1/28/98)

WINSLOW, Will C. - wife is Addie (10/24/89); with John Rau, owns/operates Fmt. Glass Works (4/14/92)

WINSLOW, Rev. William - brother of [Hugh] Walker Winslow; d 29 Jun 1900 out-of-state (7/5/00)

WINSLOW, William C. - estate is being settled since he recently dec (7/2/97)

WISE, Mrs. Henry - of 2.5 mi. SE of Gas City was raped in her home by a tramp 7 Mar 1900, tramp was arrested in Upland and is held in Marion jail to prevent his lynching (3/8/00)

WOMEN'S CHRISTIAN TEMPERANCE UNION (WCTU) -
BACK CREEK FRIENDS UNION - its organization was reported 8 Oct 1886 by Mrs. Mary E. Balch, mbr of Fmt. Union (4/29/98)
DEER CREEK UNION - will have a gospel temperance meeting in Hogston's Grove Sunday 5 Aug 1900 (8/1/00)
FAIRMOUNT UNION - mbrs include Allie Nelson, Louisa Henley, Addie Winslow, Mary W. Moore (8/8/89), Scytha Smith, Louisa Rush (2/7/96), Belle White, Nettie Jay, Rachel Lewis, and Adelia Lindley (4/2/97); a silver medal speaking contest was held at Bethel M.P. Ch. last Sunday; 1st place winner was Mildred Charles; Mary Winslow won 2nd place (9/3/97); the following was written by Ora E. Winslow-Fmt. Union was organized in 1877 as 1st WCTU in Grant Co.; dues were $0.50 until 1889 when they were $0.60; 1 Jan 1895 dues became $1.00; Band of Hope was organized prior to 1882; a Loyal Temperance Legion was organized in 1887 with, at one time, 80 mbrs; 1890 Miss Mary G. Hay organized a Young Women's Christian Temperance Union which met regularly for 3 yr (4/29/98); officers are: Pres.-Ora Winslow, V. Pres.-Millicent Haisley; Secretary-Sallie Oakley; Treas.-Florence Wiltsie (9/15/98); Margaret Ann Brown (dec) was a mbr (6/8/99)
GRANT CO. WCTU - has 10 Unions; Eunice P. Wilson is Grant Co. President (4/3/96)
INDIANA WCTU - the state Union was organized in 1874 (4/29/98)
LITTLE RIDGE UNION (HADLEY UNION) - named for the present Indiana WCTU president; formed with first meeting last wk; Mrs. Etta Daugherty, Pres.; Mrs. Stephen Scott, V. Pres.; Mrs. Amanda Hoover, Secretary; Mrs. Anna Winslow, Treas. (6/3/98)
MATTHEWS UNION - recently organized by Mattie O. Cammack and Eunice P. Wilson; elected officers are: Mrs. Alice Wharton, Pres.; Mrs. Sallie Walker, Vice Pres.; Marietta Dunn, Secretary; Mrs. Sarah Lyon, Treas. (11/10/98)
OAK RIDGE UNION - its organization was reported 8 Oct 1886 by Mrs. Mary E. Balch, mbr of Fmt. Union (4/29/98); mbrs include Mary Eaton, Edith Reynolds, Mary Bond, Susanna Hockett and Gracie Carey (6/3/98)

WOMEN'S RELIEF CORPS (auxillary to Fmt.'s Beeson Post, GAR) - is being organized; mbrs include Emma Zeek, Bertha Zeek, Mattie P. Miller, Delilah Hollingsworth, Emiley Scott, Manie Little, Mary E. Sissons, Mandy Little, Eliza Friend, Lydia Smithson, Sarah E. Worley, Pheba E. Deshon, Mollie Beals, Clara Morgan, Julia Main, Mattie Davis, Effie Davis, Hattie Cooper, Lizzie L. Deshon, Jennie W. Jones, Sallie Jones, Susie Smithson, Dixie Patterson, Mary Pickard, Elizabeth A. Powell, and Sarah H. Milner (11/14/89)

WOOD(S), A. Ward - age ca 60; long-time Liberty Twp. resident; d 24 Feb 1889, bur BC Friends Cem (2/28/89)

WOOD, F.W. - officer, Beeson Post of GAR (12/10/91); and I.N. Sluder own/operate Wood & Sluder Saw Mill employing 30 to 50 men (4/14/92)

WOOD, Marion - Fmt. area CW vet att a Vet Reunion in Elwood 6 Aug 1896 (8/7/96)

WOOD, Mrs. Mary E. - of Fmt. is sister of John Henley of Henry Co. (4/15/98)

WOOD, Mattie - see Milton McCOMBS

WOOD, Perry - owner/manager of Big Four Restaurant (2/15/00); sold his restaurant to Isaac Lemon (6/7/00)

WOOLEN, Adeline (Smithson) - b 23 Mar 1855; dt David and Elizabeth Smithson; m Edward Woolen 26 Jan 1870; sister of J.B. and Isaac Smithson; mbr BC W.M. Ch.; d 27 Aug 1891 (9/3/91; 9/24/91; 10/1/91)

WOOLEN, Edward - owns farm 2 mi. S of Fmt. leased by Kelsay Brothers to extract underlying stone (12/17/91)

WOOLLEN, Murton - is Pvt. In 160th Ind. Regmt. (12/15/98); is in camp at Columbus, GA (1/12/99); is East Branch Sch tchr (9/21/99; 9/13/00)

WOOTEN, Henry Y. - of Kokomo; lived in Howard Co. last 40 yr; brother of Isaac Wooten of Fmt.; d 4 Jul 1900 (7/5/00)

WORLEY, J.C. - f of Fmt., now of Linton, Greene Co. (10/19/99)

WORLEY, J.G. - of Fmt.; CW vet (3/28/89)

WORLEY, J.W. - owns a Fmt. grocery (4/14/92)

WORLEY, Sarah E. - mbr Fmt. Women's Relief Corps (11/14/89)

WRIGHT, __ - see Mrs. Ot EATON

WRIGHT, __ - dt b recently to M/M Van Wright (3/29/00)

WRIGHT, A.K. - and Co. Have a large tile factory 2 mi. SW of Fmt. at Wright's Station on the C.I.&E. RR (10/26/99)

WRIGHT, Mrs. Charles - dt Thomas Payne (dec) (12/10/00)

WRIGHT, E. Leona - is Earlham Coll student (4/3/96); Bachelor of Music; FFA music instructor; gives piano and organ lessons in her home at 304 S. Main St. (9/24/97); will be a performer in the 'Holiday Musicale' sponsored by the Fmt. IOOF Lodge and given in Parker's Opera House on 30 Dec 1897 (12/24/97)

WRIGHT, Elizabeth (Hollingsworth) - of Little Ridge; b Warren Co., OH 3 Jun 1828; dt Henry and Hannah Hollingsworth; 10 May 1847 m Moses Wright (dec 1865); mbr W.M. Ch.; d 2 May 1892, bur Park Cem (5/5/92)

WRIGHT, Frank - m Lizzie Winslow 4 Sept 1889 (9/5/89)

WRIGHT, Frank Leslie - b 4 Nov 1883; s Dr. P.H. (dec) and Mattie P. Wright; d 8 Dec 1889 (12/12/89)

WRIGHT, Jacob - of Little Ridge; d 21 May 1891, bur Little Ridge Cem (5/28/91)

WRIGHT, Jacob Reese - b Henry Co. 22 Jan 1839; m 1st Hannah Ann Stanfield in 1856; m 2nd 31 Oct 1867 Frances Finney; lived SW of Fmt.; d 17 Feb 1897, funeral in BC Friends MH (2/19/97)

WRIGHT, Jesse - b TN 22 Mar 1810; m in 1831 Charity Reese (dec 1859); moved to 3.5 mi. SW of Fmt. 1855; m 2nd Mrs. Hannah

Jones (dec); m a 3rd wife; mbr Friends; d 8 Aug 1899, bur Little Ridge Cem (8/10/99)

WRIGHT, Joel B. - s Jesse Wright of Penn, MI (12/29/98)

WRIGHT, Mattie - widow of Dr. Wright (4/11/89)

WRIGHT, Mary E. (Minnic) - of Fmt.; dt Michael Minnic (3/7/89)

WRIGHT, Mrs. Mattie P. - Fmt. Friends SS tchr (1/11/00)

WRIGHT, Nora - b Henry Co. 18 Sep 1868; dt J.R. and Frances Wright; d 4 Aug 1892 Fmt. (8/4/92; 8/11/92)

WRIGHT, Sarah Ann - see Sarah Ann BULLER

WRIGHT, Van - prop., Wright's Laundry (1/18/00)

WRIGHT, Mrs. Van - sister of Miss Emma Steinhizer of Michigan City (4/5/00)

WRIGHT'S STATION - 2 mi. SW of Fmt. on C.I.&E. RR (10/26/99)

YOUNG, William - 1892-93 tchr, Little Ridge Sch (8/25/92); 1895-96 Oak Ridge Sch tchr (3/6/96)

ZEEK, Bertha - mbr Fmt. Women's Relief Corps (11/14/89)

ZEEK, Emma - mbr Fmt. Women's Relief Corps (11/14/89)

ZEEK, Will - of Fmt. is brother of Charles Zeek of Jonesboro (3/8/00)

ZEIGLER, __ - b 21 May 1900; dt M/M Clyde Zeigler (5/24/00)

ZEIGLER, Clyde - att Chicago Art Sch (1/12/99)

ZEIGLER, Frank B. - and Charles C. Lyons have gone to inspect the Hoosier Mining Co. in the Florida Mts. of Idaho in which they own stock (7/20/99)

ZEIGLER, Mrs. Frank B. - dt W.E. Fellows (dec) (12/22/98)

Other Heritage Books by Ralph D. Kirkpatrick, Ph.D.

*Back Creek Friends Cemetery Burial Records
Revised Edition*

*Burial Records of Four Grant County, Indiana
Quaker Cemeteries*

*Local History and Genealogy Abstracts from*
Fairmount News, *Fairmount, Indiana, 1888–1900*

*Local History and Genealogy Abstracts from*
Fairmount News, *Fairmount, Indiana, 1901–1905*

*Local History and Genealogical Abstracts from
Jonesboro and Gas City, Indiana Newspapers, 1889–1920*

*Local History and Genealogy Abstracts from
Marion, Indiana Newspapers, 1865–1870*

*Local History and Genealogy Abstracts from
Marion, Indiana Newspapers, 1871–1875*

*Local History and Genealogy Abstracts from
Marion, Indiana Newspapers, 1876–1880*

*Local History and Genealogy Abstracts from
Marion, Indiana Newspapers, 1881–1885*

*Local History and Genealogical Abstracts from
Upland, Indiana Newspapers, 1891–1901*